INVENT WOW!
CREATE WEALTH

DON BROWN

Copyright © 2019 by Don Brown

All rights reserved.

Simultaneously published in United States of America, the UK, India, Germany, France, Italy, Canada, Japan, Spain, and Brazil.

All rights reserved. No part of this book may be reproduced in any form or by any other electronic or mechanical means – except in the case of brief quotations embedded in articles or reviews –without written permission from its author.

Invent WOW – Create Wealth has provided the most accurate information possible. Many of the techniques used in this book are from personal experiences. The author shall not be held liable for any damages resulting from the use of this book.

To get in touch with Don, email: support@inventwow.com.

Paperback ISBN: 978-1701604773

This book is dedicated to my daughter Courtney.
If I can write a book and get it published, just imagine what you can do... :)

CONTENTS

FREE GIFT	vii
Preface	ix
Where it all Began	xi
The Millionaire's Touch	xvii
My First Invention	xxiii
The Ab Roller Story	xxix
The Three Steps to Invent WOW	xliii

PART I
STEP ONE - INSPIRATION

1. The "Aha" Moment	3
2. The Search	13

PART II
STEP TWO - INNOVATION

3. The Napkin	27
4. The Prototype	30
5. The NDA	37
6. The Feedback	43
7. The Patent	48
8. The Trademark	56

PART III
STEP THREE - MONETIZATION

9. The Branding	67
10. The Test	71
11. The License	77
12. The Launch	85
The Mission	92
One Last Chance	95

Found a Typo?	97
About Don Brown	99
One Last Thing	101

FREE GIFT

Thank you for your purchase of Invent WOW. As an extra bonus, I want to give you a free gift called the Crowdfunding Checklist.

This is the exact process I used to generate over $400,000 in sales on my last KickStarter. And it's yours free. Just my way of saying thank you for grabbing my book ;)

InventWow.com/gift

PREFACE

The phone rang, and my mother was at the other end of the line. I could barely understand a word she was saying, through the combination of her level of excitement and the staticky connection from my early-generation cell phone.

"Mom, what are you talking about? I'm not at the mall right now."

That unexpected phone call led me down one of the craziest journeys of my life – discovering just what can happen when someone else makes a grab for one of your inventions. Never in a million years would I have thought that anyone would try to knock off my own invention so quickly, let alone in my own backyard, and that they would do such an amazing job that my mom could be there, not realize it was a knock-off, and be "mistakenly" excited for "my" success.

Becoming a successful inventor is about more than just having an amazing idea. The amazing idea is just the first part of the process, and if you're stuck there, like many inventors, you can end up going down a path to failure. This is a book for inventors, enthusiasts, creative people, and just about anyone who has a desire to turn their ideas into a financial success.

The absolute fastest way to become a millionaire in America is to have a WOW IDEA for a product and launch it to the world. Today, with the advent of the Internet and the advances in technology, it's even easier to experience massive success, but it's critical that you avoid the most dangerous pitfalls that so many inventors don't know about.

Before we dig any further, I want to share something with you, so that even if you only read the introduction and don't read the rest of the book, I save you from the biggest inventor's pitfall. If you think design or utility patents, inventor notebooks, or mailing a letter to yourself will protect you from people stealing your invention ideas, you are dead wrong. In fact, sometimes it's the complete opposite.

First and foremost, it's crucial that you come up with a WOW IDEA and turn that into a WOW PRODUCT. Before even entertaining patents and attorneys, perfect your WOW IDEA so that when you manufacture your WOW PRODUCT, you can tweak it and make your prototype functional and perfect. Let me explain why you need to do this first before diving into patents and paperwork.

A patent is nothing more than a piece of paper that gives you the right to sue people. And if you have a WOW IDEA, you will get knocked off, no ifs, ands, or buts about it! One thing this book will teach you is how to protect your WOW IDEAS with and without a patent – you will learn how to outsmart the knock-offs and stay one step ahead of them so you can dominate the market and reap the rewards of your invention without paying lawyers all your profits to sue people.

While I'm going to dig very deeply into this critical step and how you can protect yourself for just a few hundred dollars by properly filing a provisional patent application later in the book, for now, I want you to know that if you have a WOW IDEA, you will get knocked off; but at least, when you get a call from your mom, when she sees someone else at the mall shooting a video for a product they didn't invent, you will know exactly how to outsmart invention thieves.

WHERE IT ALL BEGAN

When people look at my trajectory, they assume I've always been successful. I'm known as "the Ab Roller Guy," and there's one in nearly every garage, basement, weight room, and exercise facility around the world. In fact, my copywriter lives on one of the smallest islands in the world, deep in the Third World, and even on his tiny island in the middle of nowhere, they have an Ab Roller at the gym on the beach. Don't let my biggest success fool you. I come from very humble beginnings, and I'd like to take you on my journey.

When I was only ten years old, I believed there were two ways to become rich: you were either born rich, or you had a family member who would someday leave you a fortune when they died. I grew up with the worldview that there was no other way to change your economic situation, even in the United States. Although people have always talked about, believed in, and shared the American Dream, I grew up just a little bit too rough to even consider that a possibility for me. The one hope that I gleaned from television was that maybe a rich uncle who my mother had possibly forgotten existed would die and bequeath his estate (and hopefully also his mansion) to our family. Alas, this hope was just that – a dream – so my life did not change for the better so easily.

My mother became pregnant at fourteen and never finished high school. If you think that sounds young now, it was even younger back then. And yet, less than a year later, she was pregnant again – this time with me. My older sister and I are less than a year apart. We're what some people consider to be "Irish twins."

I look at my daughter now, who's just turned twenty and is dealing with college. She's grown up in a totally different universe. I can't even imagine her with a child, and yet my mother had two by the time she was sixteen.

I'd love to say that we had a magical childhood, but we grew up a little closer to a Charles Dickens novel than I normally like to admit. My mother struggled in life, going through three different husbands and consistently working two or three jobs to pay the bills and keep food on the table. I spent my first five years growing up in a trailer in Paterson, New Jersey, with my grandparents. I never met my father. He disappeared before I formed a single memory, and when I was five, my mom met her second husband and quickly had three more children.

At the ripe old age of thirty-two with five kids, she realized she wasn't happy with that relationship. My stepdad was a drunk, and he did not treat her the way she deserved to be treated. Nobody wants their mom to be treated poorly, and it breaks my heart to think about what she went through to give my siblings and me a better life.

I was seventeen when my mom decided she was done with my stepdad. She decided the guy she had met at the bar where she worked was a better choice, so she took my younger siblings and moved in with her new boyfriend. My older sister was able to move in with her boyfriend at the time, so I was left, a seventeen-year-old about to graduate from high school, in a foreclosed house, doing my best to survive. I managed to stay there for about three months until the pipes froze. Eventually, I did get a little help from an uncle – not in the form of a million-dollar inheritance, but he was willing to let me help pay the rent at his apartment. I graduated from high school and switched from part-time to full-time working in a supermarket.

Something about growing up without enough money at the end

of the month leaves an impression on a young man, and the thought of working in a place that always had food every single day provided me with a sense of both financial and emotional security. If you work in an office or for a company that makes non-essential things, you could be laid off should that company go out of business. But I figured that the last place to go out of business would be a place that provided food for people.

My very first job was bagging groceries and pushing shopping carts at a ShopRite supermarket in New Jersey. I started working there when I was fifteen because I needed money for a car. I needed a way to get to and from school, and I couldn't rely on gifts or financial support from mom. She was struggling just to take care of my younger siblings and her new boyfriend, who loved his beer. I worked for $2.30 an hour. In my senior year of high school, struggling in between a house with freezing pipes and moving into an apartment, my guidance counselor advised me to consider a special program called "distributive education." With this program, I only attended three classes at school – English, Gym, and DE – and I would leave at 10:30 every day, heading straight from school to my job at ShopRite.

While everyone talks about how important an education is, when you're struggling to pay the rent, making it to work is just a little bit more important. When you're in the distributive education program, they prepare you to enter the workforce. They see the value in letting you start to work young and get experience, rather than taking advanced math classes and learning skills that you'll never use. For people like me, college was never an option. It wasn't even on my radar. And the fact that my daughter is in a private college right now (paid in full by me) is an absolute testament to the power of WOW IDEAS.

When I turned eighteen, I took an apprenticeship in the meat department because that was where the "big money" was, and you didn't have to wear a tie. You couldn't work there until you were an adult, and the second I turned eighteen, I wanted to get to that next level. Meat cutters made a lot more than $2.30 an hour, and that's what I wanted – a big raise.

But seven years into my meat-cutting career, the meat cutter union went on strike. They decided that we needed a better contract; the grocery store wasn't paying us enough. I never understood why we had to go on strike. I was a twenty-four-year-old meat manager making $40,000 a year, and I had things pretty good. But when your union goes on strike, you don't have a choice, so I went back to making even less than I had been pushing around shopping carts in the parking lot. I was stuck making forty bucks a week carrying a picket sign. It was January, I was freezing my butt off again – reliving memories of my frozen house from childhood – and I knew my bills would fall behind if I didn't figure out a way to bring in more income. The good life seemed to have disappeared. Marching with that picket sign in my hands, the freezing wood against my knuckles, I knew I had to do something, so I applied for a part-time job at a local gym – a decision that would transform my life forever.

At that point in time, I was only doing two things in my everyday life: I cut meat, and I worked out at the gym.

I started lifting weights at the tender age of ten years old, after seeing an ad in a magazine of Charles Atlas with big muscles. I also loved watching Jack LaLanne on television. He was the first one with a TV exercise show. LaLanne was one of my idols as a little kid, and I was excited to supplement my picket-line income with a part-time job at a Jack LaLanne Nautilus Center in Chester, New Jersey.

At that time, I didn't have a home phone number, so I had to write down the office number of the supermarket on my applications. One day, I was out there, freezing and shivering, picketing my way through a cold, cold winter, when one of the cashiers walked out from the supermarket, saying, "You've got a phone call. There's a Jack LaLanne fitness center calling you." I actually walked in from the picket line, which, normally, you're not supposed to do ("crossing the line"), but in this case, it was just to take a phone call. And that's how I began my career in the fitness industry.

I started working at the gym during that strike, but when the strike ended, I didn't give up my second career. The only thing better than one job was two jobs. If there's one thing I learned from my mother's struggles through life, it's that you have to depend on yourself. And when you have something good going, you don't just let it go.

I would work from five or six in the morning until four in the afternoon every single day at the supermarket, cutting meat. Then, I would teach fitness from five until ten at night. Every Saturday, I had to work at the supermarket no matter what. If you were going to miss your shift at the supermarket on a Saturday, you better die or get married, because by Monday, you'd be fired. But on the occasional Sunday where I didn't have a shift at the supermarket, you could find me at the gym, putting in as many hours as I could.

For two years, I considered my work at the gym to be my vacation. Every time I had time off from work, every time I wasn't on the clock at the supermarket, you could find me either at the gym or traveling to acquire fitness certifications. Way back in the ancient 1980s, certifications were just starting to become something in the fitness industry. I was a man who had barely graduated high school, with no chance of a college degree, so I worked my tail off to save the money needed to get certified as a fitness specialist with the Cooper Clinic in Dallas, Texas.

THE MILLIONAIRE'S TOUCH

My mother's advice to me and my four siblings was to work hard to graduate from high school so we could get a good job, work at that job for thirty years, and someday, we could grasp that brass ring called a pension and retire. My mother became pregnant at such a young age that graduating high school seemed like an impossibility for her. She wanted her children to have the security she didn't have – just as I graduated high school, so I want my children to go to college. We always want a little something more to protect our children, and my mom's idea of our protection was for us to work for a company that would someday give us a pension. That advice was working for me, until one night while working at the health club, a self-made millionaire changed my life.

When you look at the town where I grew up, it's kind of amazing how I could drive just a short distance from my below-middle-class neighborhood and travel through beautiful houses to the gym where I was working. The transition from inexpensive, lower-income housing to upscale clientele was both abrupt and kind of shocked me every single time I drove to the gym.

In the thirty-minute drive from the grocery store to the Jack LaLanne Fitness Center, you went from a neighborhood where people were earning $30,000 a year to one where people were earning well over $100,000 a year. While that may not seem like a lot of money today, believe me, that second neighborhood was pretty nice compared to the first one. They were earning three times as much as the families in the neighborhood where I was living. Every Sunday afternoon, after closing the health club, I would amuse myself by driving through those upscale neighborhoods. I remember some of the mailboxes being the size of mini houses.

On this particular night at the gym, a self-made millionaire and small business owner who lived in a neighborhood that I could only dream of handed me a cassette audiotape to listen to. It was a tape by Earl Nightingale called *The Strangest Secret*; he also gave me a book by Og Mandino, *The Richest Man in Babylon*. He told me, "You need to feed your mind with good stuff." He was right. That audiotape and book changed my life with a simple message: "You become what you think about all day long."

Before we complete my story, I want you to spend a moment thinking about that. What do you spend all day thinking about? As you get older, more and more of your friends go on different business, financial, and romantic trajectories, and you can see exactly what I'm talking about. The person who spends all their childhood thinking about medical school, being a doctor, and saving lives, eventually will have that thought manifest into a career.

I spent my whole childhood thinking about not having any money and hoping I would get through high school and latch myself onto a career that would last. Because no matter how much technology and the world was changing, and I certainly had no idea the Internet was coming when I was growing up – I wish I invented that! – I knew that grocery stores were here to stay. No matter how much the world changes, people still need to eat.

The content I learned from that cassette tape and book changed my life, and I realized it was time to focus on what I really wanted in life. From the outside, and based on my mother's advice, I had already achieved everything by my mid-twenties. I had graduated from high school, and I had a secure job at a grocery store with a pension waiting down the line and a union watching out for me. I even had a bonus second job at the gym providing additional income and keeping me so busy I didn't have time to spend any of that money. I was already the embodiment of all my mother's advice, but it wasn't what I wanted; I was not happy having someone else tell me what to do every day. And I'm sure it's not what you want from your life either.

From that night forward, I became a bit of a cassette tape junkie. I began investing in learning by listening to tapes recorded by Nightingale, Conant, and Tony Robbins that I purchased from a catalog. I loved Tony's cassette program called *Personal Power*; I even ended up walking through fire at a Tony Robbins seminar, and all the amazing things you can do to empower yourself – especially the idea that you can believe in yourself enough to affect your situation in life. I was surrounded by successful people at the gym every day, helping them train, and I started to realize it was possible for me to transition to the other side of the glass. I could be more than just an observer to their lives; I could become one of them.

After nine and a half years working as a meat cutter, just six months away from my tenth anniversary, where I would secure my first pension, I decided to quit that job. I did the exact opposite of what my mother told me to do. I said goodbye to the pension and jumped at the chance to own my own business.

As I was training people at the gym and listening to my motivational tapes, I always had this thought in the back of my head that maybe I could own one of these places, that maybe I could be an owner or partner, rather than the guy out front, grinding for a paycheck. When the opportunity came to not only to own a gym but to own and take over *that* gym, I jumped at it.

Every Sunday night, after closing down the gym, checking the locker room, and locking all the doors, I would sit down at the manager's desk and say, "Someday, I'm going to own a place just like this one." And then suddenly, I did.

The health club where I'd worked part-time was going out of business. Rather than seeing this as a warning sign, I saw it as an opportunity. I could run this place better than the last owners. It was now or never. The gym was shutting its doors because it couldn't keep up the sales volume, the staff was upset that they were losing their jobs, and the voice of Earl Nightingale whispered into my ear, "You can save all their jobs. You could turn this place around. You can become whatever you think you can..."

When that gym went out of business, the creditors stripped away everything. All they left was the carpeting and the mirrors, but at least the building was already built like a gym. It had a foundation I could work with. The plumbing was in the right places, and that was a big advantage.

I took every single penny I had – $40,000 that I'd saved over my nine-year career as a meat cutter and part-time gym instructor – and put it down as a security deposit to lease the building and order some Nautilus machines for the gym. But by the time we opened the doors, all my money was gone.

I somehow convinced one member from the original fitness center to help me secure a loan for $50,000. He put a mortgage on his house in exchange for eighty percent ownership of my business, which he wanted to hold as collateral until I paid him back. He was an attorney and looking back at that deal, I should never have given up full control.

When you hear the first part of that story, it's amazing to know that someone was willing to risk their home and fifty thousand more dollars to invest in me starting a business. However, on the other side of the coin, when you think about him owning eighty percent, I'm sure you can understand that owning that gym was never going to make me a millionaire. I was only keeping one out of every five dollars of profit that came through the doors. I didn't care if it was a bad deal. I didn't know what I was doing; I just knew that I wanted to run my own business, and I was about to lose everything.

I almost went out of business many times because I had no clue what I was doing. But that was my first shot at entrepreneurship, and I was running my own show. Since 1986, the year I quit my job at the grocery store, I've always been independent. Somehow, I'd always figure out a way to make money; a couple of years would go by, and I'd get this big hit, and then this belief that just goes back to saying, "I could become rich; I should be focusing on what I want, not what I don't have; that desire will manifest."

Long before people started calling it the "Law of Attraction" or the "Secret," Earl Nightingale had already revealed it with "The Strangest Secret," a gold recording which made it very clear: you become what you think about all day long. I was focusing on getting to the next level and making my dreams come true. I can tell you that when I get into bad deals, and I start focusing on the money I'm losing and the way things are going wrong, that cycle gets worse and worse. But it doesn't have to.

My story would have ended with someone struggling to make a living owning a gym if it wasn't for the power of positive thinking, invention, and taking action.

MY FIRST INVENTION

I wish I could tell you that my first invention was a massive success and that I knocked it right out of the park, but the truth is, if you want to live the dream, you have to endure a few nightmares first. And while my first idea was a good one, I made some critical mistakes that prevented me from earning a dime off that idea.

When I first took that job at the health club, my assignment was to walk people through the room, show them how to use each of the machines, and just be there as a strength coach, making sure that everyone was using the machines safely. I was helping people to work out, measuring them, weighing them, and helping them to track their progress.

Then, one day, the rules changed. A new manager came in and said, "Everyone has to participate in the group exercise or dance classes." Aerobics was well outside my area of expertise, and dancing was like public speaking – i.e., I would rather die – and while I tried to talk my way out of it, my new manager was adamant.

I was freaking out and terrified. Teaching people one-on-one was okay, but standing in a classroom with a big mirror at the back and the glass where everyone in the other room can watch me? I didn't know if I could handle it. This was back when you had to make your own cassette tape using vinyl albums to prepare the music for the classroom – iPods and CDs hadn't been invented yet. I didn't know a thing about the music to put together for a workout program. Fortunately, one of the girls who was teaching the dance class helped me, even though I was a complete wreck.

I had to teach a group fitness class they called "Cal Aerobics" or "Calisthenics/Aerobics." It was all jumping jacks, push-ups, and squats – basically, it was very similar to the things you do these days in a CrossFit program. It amazes me how everything in health and fitness comes full circle. We go from low fat to Paleo, from high impact to low impact, and then back to high-intensity training.

Every single day, I would have butterflies in my stomach before class. I would come out of the locker room, and all these people would be waiting for me, expecting a great class. I was so far outside my comfort zone; it was unbelievable. We were jumping on concrete floors with a little carpet on top back then, and everybody had their share of shin splints, but they didn't care – the high from a great workout was always worth the pain of exercise. No pain, no gain.

Every Tuesday and every Thursday, for thirteen years, this was my life. I had the most popular class, and I continued teaching classes throughout my entire career at the gym. That changed my life because it forced me to grow as a person.

I suddenly understood the power of helping larger groups of people. You can influence a few people a lot, or lots of people a little bit. I started to realize that, by helping larger groups of people, I could make a bigger difference in the world.

These people were incredibly grateful, and it made me feel good. You change people's lives when you get them in shape and when you care about them – when you give them a reason to come back every single day. Most people don't even have the motivation to get out of bed, yet we had classes at five and six in the morning, and people were lining up in the parking lot.

There's one critical difference between how I ran the gym and how it was run before I took over. The old gym was focused on one thing: sales. Sell as many lifetime memberships as possible. Once someone paid for a lifetime membership at the gym, the owner didn't care if the customer ever came back to the gym. None of that mattered anymore because the financial transaction was finished. The owner had their money, and that's all that mattered. But I knew it was a business model doomed to failure.

While all they cared about was making money, I cared about helping people get results. And I figured out that if I worked on giving people amazing results, the sales would follow suit; people would stay for far longer and would gladly pay for a monthly membership. And when all their friends saw their amazing results, they would join the gym too. This is how I successfully ran a gym for twenty years, even though I started from knowing almost nothing about business.

During this time, I had my first inspiration for an invention. It seems almost shocking now, but back then, there was no easy way to check your pulse to determine if you were working hard enough to get results. We had a giant clock on the wall, and everyone would look at it and try to count their pulse and watch the second hand at the same time. People would come up with crazy numbers that made no sense and did nothing to help them monitor their workout intensity. I knew there was a problem. The last thing people want to do is work on their multiplication tables while they're trying to have a workout.

As I was thinking about this problem for my students, I remembered Tony Robbins saying, "Ask the right questions and you will get the answer," and, "There must be an easier way. There must be a better way."

I was driving back to the gym the next day, and as I went through a traffic light, I had an epiphany. I said to myself, "What if I used the three lights of a traffic light as a system? The light turns yellow to prompt people to get ready. When it turns green, you start counting your pulse, and when it turns red, you stop. Instead of trying to count seconds and the hand of the clock, all you had to do was count the number of beats from green to red; we could have a much simpler system, and people would find it a lot easier. They wouldn't have to deal with the stress of watching the little arm go around the clock and trying to figure out their calculations. They could just follow the stoplight.

I took it one step further and created a pulse count chart showing them where they needed to be. The time from green to red was ten seconds. If you were a thirty-year-old and had twelve beats from green to red, the chart would show you exactly where you should be, and you could adjust accordingly. No multiplication needed.

That's how I came up with my first invention and created a product called the Pulse Light. I had no idea what I was doing, but I designed in my head what I thought it would look like. I was so proud. It was my first invention, and it was a WOW IDEA. People loved it.

For the first prototype, I bought a cheap plastic traffic light meant for the roads, and I had an engineer friend help me convert it into my invention. He was a member of the health club, and he helped me program a little chip so that it would stay green for ten seconds and then switch to red. The problem was if you didn't catch it right at the yellow, you had to wait another ten seconds, and your heart rate would slow down, so your numbers wouldn't be accurate.

I discovered a small problem, and I needed to make one improvement, so I invented a set of dual lights. They looked like two peace signs. One would be slightly ahead of the other, so if you missed one, you would just use the other set of lights to check your pulse. Nowadays, of course, we have chest straps and Apple Watches, and it's easy to monitor your pulse, but at the time, there was nothing at all like that. What seems like nothing now was an amazing revolution back then. And that was my Pulse Light.

My big mistake was that the manufacturing cost was way too high, and that killed me. I went to trade shows and sold quite a few, but in the end, I lost $70,000 on that invention - $20,000 of which was from my own personal savings.

I had skin in the game, and I lost it all. It wasn't that it wasn't a great idea; it was that I didn't have all the Invent WOW steps in place yet. I did not understand the "rule of five" of manufacturing. I didn't understand the difference between what it costs to make something and what people are willing to pay for it. That's a critical concept that I'm going to cover in great detail in just a little bit.

Today, that same product would be incredibly cheap to make. With LED technology, the cost of colored lights has dropped through the floor. I could have made it for five bucks instead of the two hundred it cost me per unit back then.

The Pulse Light was my first WOW IDEA and the first product that I took out into the world, and it failed due to a classic mistake that most people make. People over-engineer, over-manufacture, make stuff out of the wrong material and make things too complicated. We can have a great idea, and then something goes wrong in the follow-up step and keeps us from the success we deserve.

It's those unknown yet simple steps that I'm going to cover in great detail throughout this book to help every potential inventor, engineer, and anyone excited about building a product out there to ensure you maximize your odds of success.

THE AB ROLLER STORY

Losing my own money was bad enough, but I felt even worse about losing the $50,000 in other people's money. Most people would pull up their tails and just quit and give up. I'll admit – that was a very tough day. Failing with my first big idea was not easy. I thought I had created a hit product, and it totally failed. I lost real money for myself and my investors. I decided to take a short break. I took a backseat from thinking about inventions for a while because my fingers were burned. As they say, "Once bitten, twice shy."

But that feeling didn't last forever, thank God. One day, I was working with one of my personal training clients doing abdominal exercises. She was suffering from severe whiplash and a neck injury, and because of the pain in her neck, she couldn't do a sit-up or a crunch. I began to think about this problem – there had to be a way for her to do a sit-up using her abs without also engaging her neck.

You're not supposed to use your neck in a sit-up, we all know that, but when you perform an unaided sit-up, it is next to impossible to eliminate all neck engagement. That's why she couldn't work on her abs; the slightest pressure from her neck injury was holding her back from performing sit-ups. We tried loads of different ways of supporting her head, such as putting a towel or an ankle weight behind her head. I thought that if there was a way to support her head effectively and totally eliminate any pressure on her neck, then she could get great results from these workouts – as much as everyone else.

I was sitting in my office – that same manager's office I'd always dreamed of sitting in years earlier – and began fiddling around with a paper clip. As I was bending the paper clip, I bent it into a shape similar to a small rocking chair and started rocking and rolling it on the desk, forward and back, and I thought to myself, "Can it be this simple? Oh my gosh, I think this could work!" I instantly had a vision of how I could solve her problem. I realized that if I just built a frame around her body, I could solve her problem of neck strain while doing a sit-up. I knew right then it was my next WOW IDEA!

At that moment, my bookkeeper walked in and saw me staring at a paper clip, as though I was holding up the Holy Grail, and she said, "What's that?" I responded, "This is going to make me a millionaire." She probably walked out of my office, thinking I was crazy, but three years later, I actually became a *multi*-millionaire because of that WOW IDEA, and it all started with a bent paper clip.

At the time, I knew nothing about manufacturing, working with prototyping companies, or any of those "technical" things. I knew how to work with my hands. I was very good at that. I took my tiny paper clip model and immediately went to Home Depot to buy pipe, some pipe insulation, and duct tape. With just a few supplies, I made a full-scale version of the miniature paper clip. I laid it on the floor in my garage, I tested it, and it worked perfectly – perfect sit-ups without any neck engagement. I couldn't believe it. My invention actually solved the problem.

I didn't realize it at the time, but this was a very important step that is so critical for new inventors: I made a successful, working model of my idea, I didn't merely make a drawing. Next, I wanted to see if others liked my invention, so I had my attorney create a document called a nondisclosure agreement (NDA) for protection. Think of the document they make you sign when you become a spy, promising never to tell a secret; that's what an NDA is.

I started bringing in people; they would sign the NDA, and I would show them my idea. I got loads of feedback, and everyone loved it, but they also gave me a few tiny tweaks that made it work even better. There is nothing like having real people telling you how to make your product better. Then, one of my personal trainers tried it. He was blown away and begged me to let him invest in it. I was so busy running my health club that I said okay. If you can invest some money, I will let you in.

At this point, let's take a step back and summarize what happened so far in my invention process: I identified a real problem, I visualized a solution, created a mini-prototype, built a real working prototype, solicited real customer feedback, and made minor modifications to my prototype. I also found a partner and investor. Next, it was time to make a full-scale professional version.

I knew a guy from my gym who worked at the USGA; he was an engineer and understood angles and how to describe radius etc. He was the guy who approved golf clubs and golf balls for professional golf, so he was an excellent resource. After he helped me do a rough drawing on paper as a crude version of a blueprint, I was off to a local pipe bender who made the first "Ab Roller" frame out of stainless steel.

Remember the personal trainer who wanted to become my partner? Well, he borrowed $20,000 from his family to invest in my idea. I was blown away. There is nothing like having someone invest money who is as excited as you and willing to work around the clock to help make your invention a success.

Next, we needed to find someone to create the foam head, arm pads, and the vinyl. For these parts of the invention, I didn't go to an engineer or a fancy designer; instead, I went to a guy I knew who did upholstery.

At the end of this very blue-collar process, I had the perfect prototype; it was based on all the feedback I had received from all my test subjects. Now I was ready to show it to the right people. My dream was to sell my invention to NordicTrack. They had these amazing infomercials on television all the time selling the Nordic Gym Gold, so I got a big old VHS camera, and I painted my invention gold just like the Nordic Gym. I made it as close as possible to how their products looked to help get them excited. I wanted them to see my vision of how it would look like as part of the NordicTrack family of amazing inventions. I knew these guys would like it, so I called it the Nordic Crunch, long before I called it the Ab Trainer or the Ab Roller.

I made a short two to three-minute video of me demonstrating how it worked, showing off this hand-built, golden Nordic Crunch. I boxed up the video, and I sent it off to the corporate offices.

Finding out how to send my video to NordicTrack took a little bit of work. Remember, this was way before the Internet! I grabbed a magazine that had an advertisement for the Nordic Gym Gold, I called up the 800 number you call when you're looking to place an order, and I asked them who was in charge of new product submissions.

NordicTrack's business model at the time, at the early advent of infomercials, was to get you to call their 800 number. They would ship you a VHS tape, you would watch it, and then you'd want to buy the Nordic Gym. It would inspire you. They were mailing out infomercials. I decided to do the exact same thing back to them; I used their business model and sent them a VHS tape to hopefully inspire them to buy my invention. I finally got the name of the head of new products, and they gave me his phone number and mailing address right on that call, so I took my tape and sent it right to him.

I didn't have to wait long. Three days later, my phone rang. "Mr. Brown, we watched your video, and we want to do a deal. We'll send you an agreement right away." They were obviously excited about my invention. I had confirmation from an industry expert that I had a WOW IDEA!

In the mail, I got a contract for a royalty of four percent, and they offered me $2500 as an advance. I didn't know anything about contracts, so I went to my patent attorney, and I showed him the contract. He said, "Well, don't quit your day job, but you might make some money someday from this."

As I was about to sign the contract, my partner/employee told me that his brother-in-law was a major merger and acquisition attorney for a large law firm, and he told me, "Don't make that deal. Wait." I was fortunate, almost lucky, that there was someone in my life who knew what they were talking about and could give me expert-level advice on negotiating.

I decided to hold off, and NordicTrack doubled their offer. I thought, "Woah! This is amazing. This is the easiest negotiation I've ever done. I don't do anything, and they double it!" But when I didn't take that deal, they threatened just to copy my idea and bring it to market because I didn't have a patent yet. The very people I wanted to do business with, the company I dreamed of working with, threatened to steal my idea and rip me off.

I went back to my partner's brother-in-law, and he said, "Don't worry. I'm going to write a letter for you, and you're going to send it." If you've ever gotten a letter from an attorney, you know they know exactly how to make you feel terrible. I sent his letter to the head of NordicTrack, and it was something to the tune of, "I can't believe you threatened to rip off inventors. I thought you were an inventor-friendly company. This is ridiculous."

That letter got into the hands of somebody above the guy who said they would make their own version, and long story short, he got fired for threatening to steal my invention. NordicTrack then called me up and flew me out to Minnesota, and they offered me a lot more money. But I still didn't take it, because this mergers and acquisition lawyer kept saying, "No, just wait. There's something bigger coming around the bend."

I decided to continue on my own, so I didn't make any deal with NordicTrack and instead took my invention to a big fitness trade show in Chicago where loads of big companies like Nautilus and StairMaster were showing off their amazing products. I was there in my inexpensive little booth, far away from all the exciting, fancy booths. I didn't have any expectations because I had never attended a Trade Show before. I couldn't afford any expensive marketing or advertising budget to attract attention at the show, so I was hoping our booth wasn't empty and dead the whole time. Well, all my fears disappeared. My booth was the busiest one at the show! Even busier than the big-name fitness companies. At the time, I called my invention the "Ab Trainer." (I couldn't very well call it "NordicCrunch" anymore since I did not cut a deal.) People at the show couldn't get enough of it. I was so overwhelmed by the attention that I didn't notice all these people taking pictures of the different pages of my brochure while I was showing off my invention. That would later come back to sting me.

A lot of people told me that it was the best invention ever, and they wanted to buy it or do business with me. A huge fitness/medical company called Cybex approached me, "We want to do a fifty-fifty deal, and we'll give you a $175,000 advance." I nearly had a heart attack. These were the types of numbers I'd only been dreaming of.

The man from Cybex told me, "Look, we can build this right in New York. We make canes and walkers, and we bend pipes just like this 24/7. Our factory can easily manufacture this for you. This is right in our wheelhouse." I said, "That's great, but we have to do a TV infomercial because I know that this will dominate as an infomercial. When people see this on television, they're going to grab the phone and buy it." He said, "No problem," and they signed the agreement. He was the president of the company – he loved it. We were all on the same page.

Everything was great until three months later when the president got fired, and the CFO (Chief Financial Officer) took over. If you know anything about CFOs, they're very cautious. They're focused on the numbers, not building new products. Accountants are not known for taking risks and living on the edge, and this CFO was no different.

He invited me to a meeting and said, "Just so you know, we're not going to do an infomercial. That's not in our plans anymore. We don't like big spikes in sales that die off over time. What we like is a steady, consistent, predictable income." I said, "I completely understand where you're coming from, but the contract says you have to do an infomercial. That's our agreement."

In the end, I had to take them to court. I sued them, and they had to give me an interest-free loan for $300,000 to pay for my first infomercial. A rather circuitous path to the infomercial, but I knew that was where my invention would take off. And all the knock-offs were starting to appear on QVC and TV everywhere. I was sick to my stomach.

I quickly began to look for a production company to work with, and I found in Utah, one called Stilson & Stilson. They became famous for an infomercial for a product called the Health Rider, selling it for $400. To me, it just looked like a simple seesaw, but they were absolutely killing it with that product. I knew that we could do amazing things with my Ab Trainer, so I hired them to produce my first ever TV Infomercial.

People around the world were filing patents using pictures of my drawings from the brochure I displayed at the fitness expo to say it was their invention. I was getting copied by so many companies calling their inventions "ab roller," "ab shaper," "perfect abs," and so many more.

When you have a new idea, and you have something revolutionary, you have to protect yourself in the right way. I didn't know that back then. The story of my Ab Trainer/Ab Roller invention turned into a story of me fighting against people all over the world who were trying to steal my WOW IDEA.

I don't want that to happen to you. I don't want you to have to go through the pain that I went through. This book is the guide I wish I'd had twenty-five years ago. Learn from my mistakes so that you don't repeat them. I know you were thinking that this story was just getting so good. That it would be the story of my meteoric rise to the top with no challenges. But my life isn't a movie.

The amount of time between building my first prototype and releasing my first product kept getting extended, first by the complicated negotiations with NordicTrack, then the second round of negotiations, and finally the lawsuit which I used to fund my infomercial. All these challenges kept delaying the process, but things were finally coming together. We were about to start filming the infomercial when my phone rang. My mom couldn't be more excited. She was so proud of me. The woman who originally told me, "Just find a job where you can lock in a pension," was at the mall, watching them filming an infomercial for her son's product.

When she called me, it took a few moments for me to understand what she was talking about, because we weren't shooting an infomercial that day. My mistake at the trade show, letting people take pictures of my brochures when I was busy and distracted, meant that loads of people out there had the plans to build my device. Someone living very close to me had done exactly that, and they had the gall to film their infomercial in front of my own mother.

I ran down there to see what was going on and deal with this problem face to face. Sure enough, a local New Jersey infomercial company was filming an infomercial for a product they were importing from China. They were shooting an infomercial for my product in my own backyard, and my patent hadn't even been issued yet.

I confronted the producers at the mall, and I started screaming at them and making one hell of a scene. Then I called the owner of the company. I said, "How dare you steal my product? How dare you steal and produce a TV show in my own backyard?" He asked, "Do you have a patent?" And I replied, "Well, it didn't issue yet." He said, "Well, then, I don't believe you," and hung right up on me. And that was it. He made my blood boil and became my archenemy.

My only hope was getting that patent in my hands as soon as possible. Once it was issued, and I had that physical piece of paper, then I could prove that it was my invention and defend my WOW IDEA. But, as I'm sure you won't be surprised to learn, there were a few more stumbling blocks ahead of me. The next one was that the United States Patent Office literally lost my patent.

I called them up to check on the progress, and they said, "Oh, we can't find it." Without that physical piece of paper, you didn't have a patent. The law clearly states that your patent must be published and issued before you can accuse anyone of copying your WOW IDEA.

I went to the Patent Office in person, and I couldn't have been more shocked. There were only a couple of ladies and piles of patents everywhere – boxes and boxes in the office and in the hallways. My first thought was, "Okay. I see how someone could lose a patent in this place." There were shopping carts filled with patents, and each one had a little barcode on it. How could they ever find my patent in that disaster?

I did the only thing I could do: I called them every single day, encouraging them, supporting them, begging them, and using every single technique in the book hoping they would find that patent. I told the ladies on the phone that the world was stealing my idea, and I was going broke fast. I begged them to keep looking. After what can only be described as one of the most stressful times of my life, one fine day, the phone rang; they had found it.

But when they finally issued the patent, it was weak. They'd beat up so many of my initial claims that the patent was almost indefensible. When you file for a patent, they can pick and choose which of your claims they accept and which they reject. In my case, the patent examiner said he would not allow most of my primary claims, so I had no choice but to file an additional patent called "continuation in part." I expected the narrow claims to get a patent in my hand fast. They told me my invention was too similar to a rocking chair, so they wouldn't give me the broader claims.

I've certainly never seen anyone use a rocking chair for a sit-up, but they told me that my only option would be to fight for those claims with the board of appeals. I filed my appeal, and after six months of struggle, I went before the Board of Appeals. They gave me every single claim. The initial examiner was too afraid to give me a broad patent, so he just wimped out, and it cost me an additional six months.

If you thought I went to war to get my patent, you ain't seen nothing yet.

With the patent in my hand, I finally had what I needed – the power to sue everyone. People were making millions of dollars with something they'd stolen from me. It was time to fight and get what was mine.

I went back to the attorney I'd been working with, who had also become one of my partners, and we spent $12 million in litigation. Thank God, I was making enough money from my own infomercial to fund my legal campaign.

After the patent was issued, through a series of unexpected twists and turns, the very guy who had hung up on me and told me he didn't believe I really had a patent ended up becoming one of my most important business partners.

One of my business partners found a company in California that would agree to promote my infomercial on TV. It was a big infomercial company, and I gave them the rights to use my patent and run infomercials just like I wanted. And who did they decide to work with on the TV infomercial? The very guy who'd filmed an infomercial in front of my mom! It turns out his infomercial was selling better than my Ab Trainer.

But this is one of those stories that have a happy ending. We began partnering together, and we eventually became best friends. We're still friends today, and we laugh about it sometimes. I remind him, "You know, if you hadn't hung up on that phone call that day, and if you'd talked to me and partnered with me, we would have each made $50,000,000."

There was that much money being made on TV from my WOW IDEA. I went from a guy who'd just been cutting meat and working in a gym to one of the most successful inventors of fitness products of my generation. These were numbers that I never even imagined talking about or saying, let alone making.

There were companies in China cranking out knockoffs for $10 a unit. Even undercutting the market and making a garbage rip-off version, they were making an absolute killing. I think of that time as the "Great Litigation of the 1990s." There are even articles you can look up online and stories in *The Wall Street Journal* calling it "The Great Ab Wars." Some of the companies that were selling the product – most of them – were even using my name, and not paying me a penny. My partner/attorney became the star of his law firm because we were spending millions suing everyone out there. And I had a rock-solid patent, so we won a bunch of lawsuits.

But with that kind of money in play, sometimes even lawyers get sticky fingers. When I checked my accounting and their billable hours, I discovered they had overbilled me by three-quarters of a million dollars. If you've ever seen the Tom Cruise movie *The Firm* or read the book, you know that lawyers will even rob the mob if they think they can get away with it. They ended up discounting the remaining bills and claimed it was just an accident, blaming it all on a junior clerk making a billing mistake.

Even though that attorney initially gave me the best advice and helped me to become a millionaire, his law firm lost all my business and all my trust. I moved on, and I found another guy – an ex-attorney from Skadden, Arps, who was pumped and excited to work with me. We're still partners and working together to this day because when you find a great ex-lawyer who is also an entrepreneur, you stick with them as long as you can. Together, we finished suing many companies, including all the biggest retailers – Walmart, Target, and Kmart.

We sued all the retailers because we figured something out: retailers do all their business on a system called "plus ninety." They get the goods from the supplier, but they don't pay for ninety days. Because of the way their money is structured, they don't want to be in litigation during that ninety-day period, and it's a rolling ninety days, which makes them especially vulnerable to this type of lawsuit, so they always settle quickly.

You'd think the last person you want to sue is the very one you want to sell your product, but sometimes, you've got to send a message. And our message was, "Don't sell the knock-offs." Before we went after the knock-offs directly, we went after the distribution channels. I wanted to shut off their revenue stream as quickly as possible, and then go after the money they'd already stolen. I didn't want them using the money they made selling a knock-off of my product to pay their lawyers to fight me, so we cut them off at the knees.

All these companies that were ripping me off got a call from Walmart, Target, and Kmart that said, "Look. You've got to settle this.

We do not want to be a part of this litigation process. The last thing we want to do is be accused of selling stolen goods. You need to settle the claim with this guy right now." I turned the biggest retailers in the county into my allies because they wanted this problem to go away. They wanted to keep selling this product because they were making a killing, and so they leaned on the suppliers of the knock-offs – which worked in my favor. Millions of dollars of settlement money came in almost immediately.

One guy out of Texas had an amazing specialty distribution business selling fitness products such as dumbbells, weight benches, and barbells to many little fitness stores all over the country. He was approached by a manufacturer from China who was cranking out knock-offs of my product. He started selling his own knock-off of my invention as fast as the factory could make them. He was shipping them all over the country, and he couldn't keep them on the shelves. They were just flying out of stock.

This version was called the "Ab X." He was pumping these knock-offs out to all these fitness dealers, but he saw the writing on the wall, and so he set aside a few million dollars because he knew that someday, whoever invented this device was going to show up and sue him. He had the money ready for that. He didn't know who the inventor was, but he had a feeling that this person would find him. He was right. He built an entire business off the back of my WOW IDEA, but he made sure to take care of me when I came a-knocking. He admitted total infringement, and because he was ready and decided to just pay me rather than paying lawyers to fight me, it set a strong precedent. The other knock-off companies took notice.

After that, all the other dominoes came tumbling down. One by one, all the rip-offs went bankrupt or ended up paying me, and over the next six or seven years, I made more money suing and settling than I actually did selling the product, simply because there were so many knock-offs out there. When sales finally started slowing down and all the smoke had cleared, the company I had licensed my idea to filed bankruptcy, costing me another $9,000,000 I would never receive.

Despite getting ripped off by law firms and partners, and despite so many twists and turns in the journey and the massive litigation headache of suing companies and fighting in court, and despite having several different business partners along the path, I was still able to walk away a multi-millionaire and go on to live a life that most people can only imagine. That is the power of a single WOW IDEA.

I learned a lot of lessons from my journey and my mistakes, and that's why I'm walking you through my process here so that you can learn from my successes, but more importantly, avoid my mistakes.

THE THREE STEPS TO INVENT WOW

Now that you know my story, I'm ready to share my entire process for WOW IDEAS. I have boiled it all down to three steps: Inspiration, Innovation, and Monetization.

Inspiration is about coming up with a WOW IDEA. Innovation is about making it real and turning it into a physical product – something you can see, prove it works, and get people excited.

Finally, Monetization is how you get it out there and actually make money.

Without further ado, let's dig into Inspiration.

PART I
STEP ONE - INSPIRATION

1

THE "AHA" MOMENT

The first step in the Invent WOW system is that moment of inspiration when you see a problem that affects you or many other people, and you find a way to fix it or solve it. There are so many inventions out there that make us go, "Oh, why didn't I think of that? It's so simple." That's how you know you have an amazing WOW IDEA. It doesn't have to be complicated. My first invention simply made it easier for people to check their pulse. My second WOW invention, which changed my life, simply provided neck support while exercising their abs. I didn't cure cancer; I just helped people do a better sit-up.

In the early 1940s, a Swiss man named George took his dog for a walk in the woods. His dog was just like mine, meaning he would run around looking for trouble. My dog has never seen a bush he didn't want to sniff or a wild animal he didn't want to chase, and George's dog was no different. When his dog came back from romping around, George noticed he was covered in burrs. Those little seeds would always get stuck in the dog's fur, and that day, they were stuck in George's pants too. The hunter in him was ready to go home and embark on the task of pulling off each burr before it was embedded too deeply in his dog's fur, but the engineer in him started to wonder why these burrs were so darn sticky.

Unlike millions of other people around the world who have been annoyed by burrs pricking their fingers and getting tangled in their hair and clothing, George got curious. He took one of these little seeds into his lab and slid it under the microscope. Those little annoying burrs were covered in hooks that would catch on fabric and hair. They were designed to hook onto passing animals and travel further into the woods. Eventually, the burr would fall off the animal, and there a new plant would grow from that tiny seed.

Many plants depend on bees and wind to move their seeds around, but burrs depend on wild animals and their fur. Gazing into that microscope, George de Mestral had his "aha" moment. His catalyst was one that many others had experienced, but it hit him in that unique way. Problems, frustrations, curiosity, and entertainment are all catalysts or spark to WOW IDEAS. Burrs have been sticking to people's pants for thousands of years, but he was the first one curious enough to say, "I wonder how those actually work?" And he came up with an invention that changed the world: Velcro. Where other people saw an annoying problem, George saw opportunity. After seeing the simplicity and function of Velcro, so many other people were left scratching their heads saying, "Why didn't I think of that?"

MOST INVENTIONS these days come from a problem/solution paradigm: you have a problem, you think of a way to solve it, you start showing other people, and if your idea spreads like wildfire and everyone wants it, you know it's a WOW IDEA.

We can strip down my entire Ab Roller development from problem (neck pain while doing sit-ups or crunches) to solution (find a way to support the head and neck better). The solution can be found by asking a question: what can I create that would support the head and neck in a way that doesn't cause pain while doing a crunch?

We can look at our problem and turn it into a question to spark the idea for an invention. One of the inventions that we almost don't think about because it's ubiquitous is the can opener. Before it was invented, you opened a can with a knife-like blade that you would press around the lid. People would often get cut opening cans that way. Imagine trying to open a can with a knife right now. We know that can lead to disaster.

One day, an inventor asked a simple question, "How can I open cans in a safer way to prevent cutting myself?" And their answer was to attach a blade to a plier-type device. That was a great invention for a long time, and you'd think that's the end of the road. But no, someone else looked at that product and saw a new problem. Cutting yourself with the can opener was no longer a problem, but the lid of the can itself was now very sharp, and the blade of the can opener would get really dirty. When I grew up, can openers were quite sharp – you'd cut the can open, and you'd be left with a razor-sharp disk in the middle of your soup. People would still cut their thumbs on these can tops all the time.

While we had overcome that initial problem of, "I'm always getting cut when I'm using a knife," now we were getting cut by the lids of the can. That's how someone else came up with the idea to make the next iteration of the safety can opener, which simply provided a way to separate or delaminate the lid from the side of the can.

That first can opener was just the initial invention, followed by five or six other inventions that can simply be called improvements. Many great inventions take old products and make them better. And you better believe me that each new can opener inventor made millions. Each iteration of the can opener spread across the world like wildfire. "Why are you using that old dangerous version of the can opener? Aren't you tired of cutting your thumb open? Wow, you're using your hand and turning the crank? Why don't you just push a button and use an electric can opener?" From a simple blade to a push-button opener is proof that there will always be a better way from someone's inspiration.

The first step to creating true wealth from your ideas is to have a WOW IDEA. Most ideas are just small improvements, and being able to tell the difference is the critical step in this process. Knowing the difference between, "It's a slightly different or slightly better can opener," and, "It's different enough that you can get a patent, and it's better enough that everyone will want to replace their old one with it," is crucial.

The secret to a WOW IDEA is not just being innovative. It doesn't have to be brilliant or something that no one would ever have thought of before. Instead, it has to be something remarkable, as Seth Godin states in the book *Purple Cow* – something that gets people's attention and makes them go, "Wow!" when they see it.

Rather than being impressed by your creativity, they can see the utility of the product itself. And that's the difference. We want people to react not to you, but to the product. We want them to think, "Oh my gosh, I can't believe I didn't think of it!" They're not impressed with your brilliance; they're impressed with the product. People buy great products far more than they buy great inventors.

As humans, we learn from our daily problems and frustrations, and we will gladly pay for ways to avoid or overcome these challenges. We also love to be entertained; we don't like being bored. And that's where you can find your WOW IDEA. If you can solve a daily problem, a daily challenge, or overcome an area of daily boredom, you're well on your way to something that's going to put a WOW on everyone's face.

Another way to look at WOW IDEAS is to think of new ways to use other innovations. A few years ago, someone came up with the idea of applying strong magnets to a jewelry clasp. Instead of having to fuss with those little spring hoops, you just reach back and the magnets connect. Someone looked at that and thought, "I wonder how else I could use those magnets?" They got creative and came up with magnetic toys that connect like Legos.

Take any category of products – rubber bands for instance. How can you improve on rubber bands? "What if we made them in a bunch of different colors?" That's how the colored rubber band exploded; people liked the idea of color-coding things and started to wear colored rubber bands on their wrist as reminders. Again, we think, "Oh, that's the final innovation." But no, someone else looked at those colored rubber bands and thought, "What if all those rubber bands were molded into different shapes?" On your wrist, they would look just like a colored rubber band, but when you take them off, they magically turn into a shape of an animal or logo, and they sell for ten to twenty times more than a circular rubber band. Silly Bands became so popular that if you search for them online, the first results you see are all the different high schools that banned them. Talk about a WOW IDEA from something as simple as a rubber band. I remember reading an article that the inventor sold over $200,000,000 worth of Silly Bands.

Sometimes, the idea is simply using someone else's invention in a new category – moving something from jewelry to toy or from office supply to toy can be absolute brilliance. This comes from curiosity, "I wonder how these things work? I wonder what's possible. What else can I do with it?" Curiosity is a real driving force for some inventors. We all have a slightly different process, and that's why some people are driven by problem-solving, while some are driven by curiosity. Both are absolutely fine. As you develop your own Invent WOW process, you'll find exactly where to focus your brilliance.

The final part is entertainment. People are willing to pay a lot of money to fight boredom. Most kids in school are bored, and they're looking for ways to entertain themselves without getting caught by the teacher. It's a bit of an arms race – coming up with ways to entertain themselves without being detected. I remember when people would invent games that you could load on a calculator, back when I was in school. Nowadays, if you showed a kid a calculator-based game, they would probably laugh at you, because they've moved so far beyond that. And yet, those same kids are excited by an animal-shaped rubber band.

A great place to see what people are responding to is to look at what's working in crowdfunding. Some games raise huge amounts of money, and several of the most successful fundraising campaigns are games, toys, and entertainment-based inventions. This is how much people desire to push back their boredom. You can look at toys like fidget cubes or spinners and games like Exploding Kittens. It's such a simple card game, and yet it raised $8,000,000 because it's very entertaining. Solving the problem of boredom can be just as effective as and even more profitable than solving other problems we face in our everyday life.

❖

The Process

You're reading this book because you're somewhere on your invention journey, whether you'd love to be an inventor or you have already had a couple of ideas. I want to take you through that process, starting by focusing on a category where you have knowledge, interest, or passion. If you've been a chef for twenty years, or if you're a stay-at-home parent who does all the cooking in the house, it makes sense for you to stick with what you know and come up with innovations around that. Kitchen inventions do so well; just think about how many infomercials are built around the kitchen. Companies like Lifetime Brands are always looking for the next cool kitchen gadget.

People come up with ideas in this sector all the time. When you're in the kitchen, ask yourself, "What's my biggest problem or frustration here? What's holding me back?" My own path was mechanical things and working out in a gym. It's okay to stray from your passion but to be honest, I always seem to make more money on health and fitness products, which happens to be my passion. When you try to come up with inventions way outside your area of knowledge, it's hard to stay passionate and interested. You're far more likely to follow through with something you're genuinely interested in. Not only does your knowledge in an area matter, but your passion is critical. If you cook every day for your kids but you hate it, then you probably don't want to spend your time creating an invention for cooking. Focus on inventions and ideas that get you excited.

Before infomercials were on television, pitchmen would travel from town to town, open up their wagons, and show off their products. Even today, we still see people demonstrating products in local fairs and shopping malls. Imagine if you had to demonstrate your invention every day for the next year. If you are that excited about your product, you'll love showing it every day.

On top of passion, we also want to look at knowledge. It's easy to say, "Oh, I really love football." But if you've never played it, if you've never experienced the sport, it's hard for you to invent that next product that will revolutionize the sport. Liking something isn't the same as actively participating and experiencing it, so we do want to find that balance between passion and expertise.

The first step is to focus on the areas where you're an expert and the areas where you're passionate, and then analyze products out there that people use and look for what's missing – things that you could improve or areas where they can improve.

How Do I Know my Idea's Any Good?
Selling something is easy. Educating is hard.

If you ever watch entrepreneurial shows like *Shark Tank*, or if you've ever seen someone pitching their product and trying to raise money, the second they say anything like, "We've invented a new breakthrough technology," the investors may listen but are more likely to run for the hills.

Educating a market usually costs fifty to one hundred times more money. It can succeed, but your marketing budget changes from one to one hundred million dollars. It's hard to "educate the market." That means, first, we have to tell people they have a problem, then convince them they need your new gizmo to fix it.

The last thing you want to do is pioneer a new technology. As we all know, pioneers often get shot with arrows in the back, or in today's world, they go broke before ever reaping the rewards. This does not apply to big companies like Apple or Samsung – they have no choice but to search for the next breakthrough technology. I have been fortunate to watch some really amazing changes over the years in the music player industry. When I was ten years old, my mom had vinyl albums, and my uncle had an eight-track tape player in his car. When I was seventeen, I had a cassette player in my car. I still own a Sony Walkman, which is where the iPod came from. Every one of these changes in technology costs millions to educate and convince people they need to change what they are currently using to this new technology. Most of us (me included) do not have the cash needed to educate anyone on a new breakthrough technology that they never realized they needed.

On the other hand, a WOW IDEA is something that instantly makes sense to your target market based on what they already know. You don't have to explain it to them. As soon as they see it, they get it. Sometimes, they may need to see a demonstration, which adds a layer of complexity. That's why I'm a big fan of using video to convey your idea. Even better is if someone can look at it and go right away, "I love it. I get it." That is my litmus test. If the product does not instantly make sense to the target customer based on what they already know about the category, then you're going to decrease your chances of success.

An example of how you can have a WOW product but miss on the marketing is the Nukkles Massager. When we demonstrated this in shopping malls, people loved it; as soon as they felt it, they wanted to buy one. I decided to do a TV infomercial – I was hoping to duplicate the success of the Ab Roller, and I knew TV advertising was key to success. I created a video showing people experiencing this product in shopping malls and loving it, but when we promoted it on television, people were not responding. They could see the product working, but a massager is a product that people needed to feel. I was selling the world's greatest back rub, and the only way people would buy it was if they actually felt it. The infomercial failed miserably because it did not make sense to people unless they experienced it in real life.

Coming up with WOW IDEAS for existing categories is the fastest way to create wealth because the category already exists. Whenever you have to educate the market and create a new product category that fails to make sense instantly, then you are on your way to failure.

The Ab Roller was so successful because there was a very well-established ab exercise category, and anyone who saw the Ab Roller "got it" immediately. People could see it, and it looked just like someone doing a crunch, except it looked fun, solved a big problem, caused no pain in the neck, and looked easy to do.

Reflection Questions

1. When you had ideas in the past, which part of the idea process succeeded or let you down?

2. When you look at ideas that didn't work, can you now see why they weren't quite WOW IDEAS?

3. Make a list of the three biggest invention ideas that are swirling through your mind, and take them through the WOW IDEA test:

   a. Are they in a category that already exists?

   b. Is it a category that you're passionate about and have knowledge in?

   c. When people see it, do they get it right away, or are there additional sales hurdles?

   d. Do they have to touch it? Do they have to smell it? Do they have to see a demonstration?

   e. Do they have to be told a problem exists in the first place?

4. Analyze what we covered in this section about coming up with ideas and different ways people come up with ideas (innovation and entertainment, solving problems, and curing boredom) and ask yourself, what is your approach to innovation? What works for you? Are you someone who responds to solving problems? Are you someone who is more excited by entertainment?

Activity

Go online and look up an infomercial for a successful product. You can look at a great crowdfunding campaign, or you can look for something that was successful twenty, thirty, or forty years ago. Then reverse-engineer it and look up the way the idea came about; see if that successful innovation meets the Invent WOW criteria. Research the inventor and how they came up with the product. Did the category exist before then? Through a little research, this will allow you to confirm what you've learned in this chapter.

2

THE SEARCH

It was a rainy day at the beach, and my daughter and her friend were desperate to enjoy one of the beach's ultimate treats: s'mores. You may be more of a campfire s'mores person, but my family is all about beach s'mores. Unfortunately, the rain had turned against us. Our beach house had no fireplace, so indoor s'mores were not an option. My daughter and her friends were desperate, so they decided to toss them into the microwave. Fortunately, the marshmallows didn't achieve singularity and explode, but they did melt and get all over the place.

Cleaning marshmallow goop off of a plate is a nightmare but cleaning it off the walls of the microwave is the worst. After melting, marshmallows harden into something approaching concrete. Watching my daughter and friends clean the gooey mess in its lava state, I felt that little lightbulb snap on above my head. This was my "aha" moment. I started to think about creating a protective device that would allow you to make s'mores in the microwave without suffering the messy consequences.

Before I did anything else, I needed to check on the originality of my idea. I wasn't the first person to want to make s'mores indoors, surely? With the magic of Google, I was able to research in a way that

I couldn't a decade earlier. The Internet makes things so much easier. I typed in "s'mores maker for microwave" and scanned through the results. There were loads of indoor kits to make s'mores using Sterno or a candle, but nothing using the microwave. From that single search, another invention was born.

Way back when I started inventing in 1994, if you wanted to find out if your invention was original, or if there was already something out there with the same name or a similar function, you had to go to a selected number of libraries that had access to the patent library and look yourself or hire a patent attorney or an expert and pay around $700 to find out. It was expensive and prohibitive, and it was one of the things that held back many new inventors. But these days, things are much easier, faster, and much less expensive. Now, with a click of the mouse, we can find out that same critical information.

When you're designing a product, you're trying to solve a problem, and research is everything. As mentioned in the previous chapter, we want to make sure the category already exists. I like it when I see similar products or things attempting to solve the same problem in a slightly different way. There are so many ab devices and tools to help people do crunches; the existence of such a wide market confirms the category exists and is well-established. There is nothing more exciting than selling hamburgers to a crowd of very hungry meat-eaters.

After you come up with a WOW IDEA, we want to dig deeper, and this can be done on Amazon or Google. Google even has a section where you can look up patents, and they have almost all of the patents from the United States loaded up in their search engine. You can easily check if your idea already exists and look at that category to see how people are solving the problems. You can use the Google keyword tool to see the keywords people are using to find things they are looking for. I was working on a fitness product to help women tone up their triceps. When I did a Google keyword search, I discovered that women looking to tone their upper arms were searching the Internet with the words: "How to lose arm fat." This information will be critical later, when you market your product to the world.

Amazon's entire business is built on search and the power of the review. You can look at a similar product and read the reviews from people to see what they like and what they don't like. This gives you incredibly valuable information. First of all, you can avoid wasting your time building a product that competes with someone else's or may infringe on their intellectual property. Secondly, you can see where other people are doing well and replicate that goodness. You can also see where they're faltering and avoid those same mistakes. I love reading reviews of competing products.

Additionally, Amazon ranks every single product in their store from number one down to number twenty million, so you can look at a product and see if it's really selling. Sometimes, people see a product that has loads of reviews and make the mistake of thinking that product's doing well. There's a tool called Junglescout that gives you data to see very close estimates of the monthly sales a product is doing on Amazon. If you look at their sales, they may have been huge two years ago, but now the product (or even the category) has died. We want to check not just sales over time, but also current trends to see what's working. Amazon and Google provide so much data related to your idea that will be critical to your success.

I love to go to Walmart and see what's on the shelves because guess what? If it isn't selling, it's not on the shelves. Retail space is so valuable that any product that's doing just okay is gone very fast. Amazon will list and try everything, including products that people are selling and no one's buying because it's digital real estate. Instead of getting thrown off the shelf, your listing on Amazon will be impossible to find, and eventually, you will be out of business. Amazon rewards WOW IDEAS that sell every day. No sales? Then your listing is at the bottom of the barrel.

We can get a lot of useful information and find out about the market, our potential customers, what people want and what's selling just by going into a few stores and doing a few searches on the Internet. This time is well-spent because it's going to maximize and build on your current expertise.

I know that some people want to be pioneers and come up with the first new product in a new category and revolutionize the world. The problem is that when you're a pioneer, you are rarely the one to enjoy the rewards. When somebody comes up with a great invention, someone else right behind them comes up with a slightly better variation. That first person is locked in – they've already done their tooling and manufactured thousands or tens of thousands of units, and it's hard to change quickly. It's far better to go into a proven category and to be the innovator who's just moving forward one generation. There's a lot less risk there, and you're far more likely to have massive success.

One of my buddies is the guy behind the Copper Chef. He saw a trend that people loved (copper-colored non-stick cookware) and thought, "That's interesting." He built his own version and made it a little bit original by cleverly linking a TV chef to the brand name Copper Chef, but the product is still just a copper-colored non-stick pan. It's nothing crazy nor revolutionary; in fact, it's not even copper. It's not an invention in the sense that it's not a brand-new idea; instead, it's just a refinement of an old product (Teflon) with an awesome brand name and trademark.

What you need to do is find what people already want, and then you invent a WOW version of it. Copper-colored non-stick pans already existed, but he found a way to make it WOW by giving it a WOW name. "The Copper Chef" just really sticks in your head.

This applies to many other different ways of building a business. Whether you're writing a book or creating a product, if you go online, and no one else has made anything like it, that's a big red flag. On the other hand, if the category already exists, that's a good sign. You can find your way of solving the problem, separating yourself from the crowd and with something different enough that you can get yourself a patent or trademark and WOW people too.

I know it can be frustrating when you have an idea and discover online that someone else already invented it. The universe isn't fair. It can take a lot of bad ideas, or a lot of good ideas that other people have already thought of, until you find the one on which you build your empire. There are so many people who have this story: "Oh, I had this idea twenty years ago, but I never did anything about it, and then someone else invented my idea." It's not about the first person to think of it; it's the first person that actually goes out and does it. You have to be an action-taker. If you snooze, you lose; ideas travel around in the universe waiting for people like you and me to ask the right questions and aha – you get a WOW IDEA.

The research phase is very important because you're going to gather information and understand your market. When you know that people are already trying to solve this problem, you can say, "Does my idea create a WOW response in this category? Will people actually switch from what they are currently using to my WOW invention? Can I attract customers with these products?" People are only going to buy one ab machine at a time. "Will they buy mine instead of that one?"

We can often get that information by reading the reviews, especially the one, two, and three-star reviews. Sometimes, people will leave a one-star review for something they really like, and they'll reveal exactly the one missing feature that you can use to get your hands on the perfect product.

The Validation

Once we've passed through the phase of thinking we have a great idea and checking if the category exists, it's time to validate our idea, before we go through the process of investing time, money, and energy into it. A lot of people jump right to prototyping, and I've even seen people invest huge amounts of money on the first edition of their product and fail because they loved it so much and they wanted so badly to be first to market, that they skipped the entire validation phase. What we want to do is take each of your ideas through our validation test to confirm that it's a good idea.

It's time for the WOW IDEA test. For each of these eight features, you're going to give your product a score of one to five. The higher the score, the more likely you are to knock it out of the park.

1. Is there a large category that already exists for your WOW IDEA? Here are some further questions you can ask yourself to help you rate your idea on a scale of one to five. Does the category exist? Are people spending a lot of money in the category? How wide is the market? Each time we go down a level with a specialization, we reach a smaller and smaller market. Is this a product that helps everyone? Is this product only for men or women? That cuts your audience in half. Is this only for adults? This cuts your product in half again. Sometimes it's good to niche down to a small group, provided there is a hungry crowd of buyers.

Here is a quick example of an existing category and breaking it down into smaller niches. Body massagers is a very large category; there are electric massagers and manual massagers, there are foot massagers and back massagers. What allowed me to succeed with the Nukkles Massager was focusing on handheld massagers for giving back rubs. After doing my research, I learned that most people give lousy back rubs, and I also learned that most handheld massagers are rigid and not flexible. The Nukkles Massager solved both of those problems: it was flexible and delivered an amazing back rub.

2. Are you knowledgeable about this area? Are you knowledgeable about this industry? Are you knowledgeable about this type of product? Are you knowledgeable about this type of problem? The more your expertise can leverage into this market, the better. Why do you think doctors who invent medical products do so well? There's a great value in their expertise, and they leverage that as they move into a new market. Most of my successes have been in the health and fitness industry – a category that I am very knowledgeable in.

3. How passionate are you about this idea? As we discussed earlier, could you see yourself pitching this product in stores across the country every day for the next year? Don't believe that's so unrealistic; many great products started with door-to-door sales, or with someone going to every single department store, showing their product over and over again until someone would stock it on their shelves. Many entrepreneurs – and this is where invention transitions from idea into business – go through that struggle phase. Using the Invent WOW system, you may bypass that process and go straight to a massive crowdfunding campaign or immediately license your product, but you still need to be passionate about it to go through the tough times – because there will be tough times. You have to be willing to wake up every day and love your idea so much you would do it for free if you already were a millionaire. Rate your passion and your excitement about not only this product but also the idea of selling this product and telling people about it on a scale of one to five.

4. Can people instantly understand what your product is and what it does just by looking at it? If people can look at your product and immediately go, "I know what this is; I want to buy it," that's a five. But if your product is something they have to feel, that lowers the score. Let's say if you can demonstrate the product with a video, that's a four. If they have to touch it, we're closer to a three. If you have to go beyond that into the realm where you have to start educating people about the problem, or you're in an area of problem prevention, then you're into the realms of ones and twos. To understand this step, watch a TV infomercial without the sound and see if you instantly understand the benefits, features, and value from the offer. TV infomercial producers are masters at making sure the customer instantly understands the product's value and offer.

5. Does it solve a large problem? Here, again, we look at the size of the market, but also the size of the problem it solves. If a lot of people have this problem and desperately want to solve it, you will have a high score.

People with back pain think about it all the time. It becomes the thing they think about when they wake up and when they go to bed. I have met several people who have been in chronic back pain. Every single morning and every single evening, and in between the entire day, all they think about is their back pain. And when someone has back pain, they will spend anything to fix it – cushions, custom chairs, standing desks, and any idea that seems interesting.

When you think about using a standing desk because it might extend your life or because it looks cool, that's okay, but when it solves your back pain, it makes a massive difference. It isn't just a simple addition – it becomes a need. It's not even about want because when you have chronic back pain, eliminating back pain becomes the sole focus of your life. Finding a big unsolved problem with people looking for a solution is how WOW IDEAS create wealth.

We want to measure not just the width of your impact, but also the depth. How large is your audience, and how big is the problem you're overcoming? There are plenty of great products that overcome a small problem, and there are plenty of great products that are just for a smaller market. But the closer we get to a huge market with a big need, the easier it becomes to achieve that WOW success.

6. Cost. This is an area where I faltered with the Pulse Light, and many products have died upon this beach. Depending on where you want to sell your product, and how you want to market it, certain price points are sweet spots. Short-form (one to two minutes) infomercials want to sell their front-end product at $19.99 or less. That's the sweet spot for a direct response TV spot.

If you're going to sell it for $20, you need to be able to manufacture it for one-fifth of that price, which means $4 or less. This is the 5x rule. Your first thought, especially if this is your first invention, might be, "Oh, I'm going to make $16 profit per sale." No way. There are so many other pieces that go into the process, and every part of the process takes a little taste. Once you have it manufactured, then it has to go through packaging costs, marketing costs, delivery costs, warehousing costs and so on. All these little costs along the way add a few pennies to the total. Marketing, building a website, running ads, letting people know your product exists – all that costs money, and that's why we need that wide profit margin off the gross profit to give us a chance to get there. If you want to sell a product for $100, your goal should be to make it for $20.

Having a TV infomercial is great because it drives sales online and in retail stores – that's when it really flies off the shelves. Only ten to twenty percent of people who see your TV commercial will call in to order or go online; the remaining eighty to ninety percent will wait until they see it on store shelves.

When you sell a product to retail, they tend to pay you half what they're going to sell it for. If you're selling a product on television for $20, the retail stores will pay you $10, so now that $16 is just $6, and you still have to run those infomercials to educate the market. The rule of five will protect you as you go forward; it covers you for all these different scenarios, because retail is going to be very important, and you need that buffer to provide enough money to pay for staff, commercials, website development, and everything else that might become part of the process.

We can also look at it from cost to sales. Instead of saying, "I need to make it for one-fifth the cost of $20," look at how much it would cost to manufacture. This is a reason why many people contact factories in China and get things developed there because their prices are lower. You want to find out how much it will cost to manufacture based on how many units you want. How much does it cost per unit if I get 1,000, 10,000, or 20,000? The price will go down as you do larger runs, and that's important to know. When you look at that initial run, will people pay five times that cost to buy your product? If it costs you $23, look at it and say, "Will someone pay $115 for this?" If the answer is yes, you are on your way to a profitable WOW IDEA, and that's a five.

As the ratio goes down, so does your score. If the ratio is four to one, then that's a four; if people pay three times, that's a three.

7. Is it consumable? Great products are those that the same customer will buy over and over again. A great example of that is Breathe Right strips. It's basically a Band-Aid with a plastic spring you put on your nose that pulls open your nostrils, so you can breathe a little bit better while you sleep at night. Perfect for people with allergies. Then professional athletes started wearing them to help with their performance, thus expanding the market. Breathe Right is a great example of a consumable product because you wear it, you breathe better, you take it off, and repeat.

If your product is consumable, if people finish using it and have to buy a new one, that means your value per customer will be much higher, and that can actually make up for a lower number on the previous question.

Let's say your ratio is only three to one. You can still be profitable at a 3:1. It costs you $20 to make, but people only pay $60. You have $40 to work with for each sale. Then you get it into retail. Now you only have $10 that's coming to you; you're making $10 profit before you pay your staff, before any other numbers. Your gross profit is $10. Consumable products change the rule from 5:1 to 3:1, and if you have patent protection, you can ride the wave of a WOW product with huge profits for years and years.

What is the lifetime value of your customer? How often will they buy from you? The answer to this question will help you determine how much you can spend to acquire that customer and what the bottom line selling price has to be.

If each person ends up buying three units, now you're back up from $10 to $30. And that's just as good as if you were selling that same $20-to-manufacture product for $100. Because then, you'd be getting paid $50 for that non-consumable, and again, you end up with $30 per new customer.

8. Benefit. Many people struggle to understand this concept because this is the world of pure salesmen and marketers. Most of us think, "What does this do for me?" You want to imagine your customer and ask yourself, "What is the number one reason I would buy this product?" When we think about that, we also want to ask ourselves, "What problem does this product solve, or how does this make the customer's life better?" The big question is: "What is the perceived value?" If you have a high perceived value and a low cost to manufacture, you have a WOW product. Breathe Right strips help you *breathe* – that's worth a lot to someone with a cold or allergies who cannot sleep at night. The cost? Pennies to make; *big* profit margins.

For example, if I were to buy the Nukkles Massager, it would turn my hands into those of a professional massage therapist – I could give and receive amazing back rubs. By solving back pain, we solve a really big problem, and that's a high score on that WOW IDEA. Why do you think medicine is so expensive? Besides pain, we are also motivated by pleasure. Why do you think people pay so much for Viagra or Cialis? There's a direct correlation between the benefit and the price.

Scoring your ideas from one to five, with five being WOW, is a great way to make sure you are not wasting valuable time and/or your hard-earned money on ideas that might not be WOW IDEAS. These are the general guidelines for checking to see if your product is ready to go into the next phase, where you start interacting with people outside your head.

Reflection Questions

1. Have you ever seen a revolutionary new product that was amazing but had to explain to everyone why it was revolutionary, and then it disappeared? (minidisc players, laserdiscs, Virtual Boy, etc.)

2. Can you see how the research phase can play a major role in a start-up failure?

3. Have you had ideas in the past that you wish you'd taken action on, and then you saw someone else did, and you imagined, "What if I had all those millions?" How did that make you feel?

4. Make a list of the best places for you to do research. Do you need to do patent research? Does Amazon work best for you, or does going to places in person? For different types of products, you may

need to go to different, specialized retailers. Start to make that list now.

5. When looking at your past inventions and ideas, have you let emotions guide you in the past? When using this score system and applying logic to this part of the process, can you see the value in sifting rather than just getting driven by excitement?

6. Are you excited and hopeful for the future because now you can take your ideas through a process that involves logic and systems and moves you from idea towards profitability?

Activity

For this activity, you're going to be very proactive, and we're going to continue building on our lessons from Step One. If you have one, two, three, or even ten ideas that you feel are WOW IDEAS, for each of those, you're now going to go through a research process. You can go through the websites and research sources as we discussed in the previous section, in your reflection questions. I always recommend starting with a Google search, then going to a physical store (if it's a product sold in stores).

As you go through the research, you want to ask yourself some critical questions:

1. Does this category exist?

2. Are other people trying to solve the same or a similar problem?

3. Are the other products in this category selling well or making good money?

PART II

STEP TWO - INNOVATION

3

THE NAPKIN

In 1971, a chemist named Paul was eating that classic American meal – the hamburger. Reaching for the ketchup, he had a moment of inspiration. He wondered if recent discoveries with magnets could be used to convert magnetic resonance into images. Sitting in that cafe, Paul started sketching out his idea on the only material he had available – his napkin. He imagined using nuclear magnetic resonance to look inside the human body without having to cut it open.

His idea went far beyond the x-ray, and thirty years later, Paul Lauterbur was awarded the Nobel Prize for his work in developing the MRI. The next time you're at the hospital getting a deep scan, you can smile knowing that it all started forty years ago on a ketchup-stained napkin.

Nothing excites people more than seeing a real, physical product – something they can hold in their hands or see demonstrated. There are many "invention guidance" companies out there promising to help you that say, "You don't need a patent. You don't need to make a prototype. You can just start with a simple digital drawing or have something online and show it to people." While that can work, it's not the Invent WOW system, and it doesn't maximize your odds of success. The occasional idea can work that way, but we want a process of innovation where we develop and maximize our product into something WOW which has a strong patent that can give us protection for the next twenty years. You can make a lot because the further down the Invent WOW process you go, the higher the reward will be for you. You can make a lot more money when you have a real product and show proof that people are actually willing to buy it.

In this phase, we are going to transform that idea in your head into a workable prototype, and the first thing to do is the napkin sketch. Again, I'm dating myself a little bit here, because not everyone is at a bar with a cocktail napkin when they have their idea.

Nowadays, everyone has an iPhone or an iPad with them, but you want to start by drawing your idea. This is the first step in taking it from your head into the real world. And here's why: if you're going to have someone else build it – just like I had someone else build and bend the pipe for my Ab Roller – you want to hand off a complete idea. This will also help you to see it outside of your head. The quickest way to move an idea from your head into the real world is just to draw it. It doesn't matter if you're a good artist or a bad artist – you'll be able to express your idea, and that brings you a little further down the path.

There are lots of digital programs and apps that can help you – like Sketchup or Swift Publisher, my personal favorite. If you're good with CAD, Photoshop, or Adobe products, all these different products can help you. The reason we go through this process is to solidify your idea. When you have an idea that you simply explain to people, and then they give you feedback, you don't know what they're visualizing. There's a possibility, and it's very likely, that your idea is getting lost in translation, and we don't want to leave any room open for that. We want your idea to be crystal clear, so get it out of your head and on paper.

❖

Reflection Questions

1. Has someone told you about an idea they had, and then when they showed you that idea, it was completely different from your visualization?

2. Has this ever happened when someone was describing a person – they told you what their new boyfriend or girlfriend, or someone from school or work looked like, and then when you met that person, they were nothing like your imagination?

3. Can you see the value of doing something real, going beyond just having an idea in your head and making something that is touching your body in the real world?

4. Are you starting to get excited that you've now begun your prototyping process? It can seem simple, but this is a critical step because we've moved from thinking into doing. This is the "do" and "build" phase.

❖

Activity

In your notebook, where you're keeping track of your WOW IDEAS, take each of your ideas and draw it out. It may take multiple sketches, you may have to draw arrows to demonstrate the movement, and you may have to draw and explain different parts of your image. The more detailed and more steps in your drawing, the clearer it will be to each person you show it to. We want it to make sense at this stage, because the clearer your drawing is, the more you're taking ownership, and the more proactive you're being. And this is going to help you as you move forward into each of the next steps.

4

THE PROTOTYPE

Several years ago, I was getting a hot stone massage at Canyon Ranch Spa, and I couldn't help but notice that the massage therapist kept placing the stones (river rocks) in hot water to reheat them. I asked why, and she told me that some stones are the perfect size and hold heat very well while others are very thin and lose heat quickly. My creative mind immediately kicked in, and I had a WOW IDEA. What if I could create a rock that was the perfect shape and could hold heat longer than river rocks? The next day, I did my research and found that soapstone is used as ice cubes in Finland and for wood-burning stoves in Sweden due to its amazing thermal properties. It's also non-porous, so it does not absorb liquids or human sweat. A win-win. I ordered a box of massage stones and had a therapist pick the perfect size. Next, I googled "soapstone" and found a guy in India who was willing to hand-carve 40.000 stones in that perfect shape. I named it LAVA ICE – a hot and cold therapeutic massage stone. My cost was $0.024, and we sold them in mall carts for $20 each. Take that, Pet Rock.

After completing my search for making s'mores in the microwave, it was now time to turn that WOW IDEA into a WOW product, and the first step was to prove my idea would work. My WOW IDEA was to create a container that would hold a sandwich made of two graham crackers, a piece of chocolate and a marshmallow together while the microwave heated up the marshmallow and chocolate. Besides holding the s'mores sandwich together, I also wanted the container to be clear, so you could watch it happen in the microwave. I made several napkin sketches (actually, I used my computer and Publisher). My first prototype was a glass butter dish. It worked perfect. Next, I created a plastic base.

Drawing something is great, and it will get your creative juices flowing, but that's just the beginning. You want something three-dimensional. Depending on your type of innovation, you may go through a miniature phase, or you may go full-size right away. Some people get cardboard, a pair of scissors, and some tape, and they start cutting and building the full-size version as soon as they have the drawing. There is nothing like seeing your 2D drawing become something you can touch.

In most cases, I like to create a miniature prototype first, and there's a value in the miniaturization phase too because it helps you with cost control. You can build a miniature version at a much lower cost compared to building a full-size version, and that allows you to see if it works the way you think without wasting too much money. It can save you the cost of making a full-size prototype that's not right.

Most products and innovations go through multiple prototype phases. You build a prototype, you test it, you show it to people, you get feedback, and then you make another prototype. By starting with the miniaturization phase, you significantly cut down the cost for this phase.

Imagine you're building a product, and the full-size prototype is $1,000, but you can get a miniaturized, tabletop-size version for just ten percent of the price – $100. Going through ten prototypes to get to the final prototype that you're ready to show to people would cost you $10,000 with the full-size version. But with smaller prototypes, it would only be $1,000. And then, when you make the final full-size version, you spend $1,000. You've spent $2,000 and saved yourself $8,000 in the process of getting to the perfect prototype.

If the final product is going to be small, it doesn't make sense to have a tiny version of it to show to people. It only makes sense if we're thinking something big; in that case, we want to make it something that can fit on a table.

My goal through this prototype stage is to minimize your cost. I have seen companies and inventors burn a lot of money in this stage, and I want to protect you from that as much as possible. While it's okay to go all-in on an invention when you know you have a big WOW IDEA, every penny you save now is a penny you can spend later on marketing and generating revenue. We want to control our costs from the very beginning. Even though you might be really excited, and you got all fives when you validate your idea, it's still worth controlling cost. We don't want to spend money if we don't have to.

There are lots of ways to make a prototype. I'm a blue-collar guy, and I come from a world where I work with my hands, so most of my initial prototypes are made from stuff I buy at Home Depot.

Your first prototype doesn't have to be beautiful. We'll talk about form later. For now, we want to focus on function. If it's a prototype you can build yourself, go to Home Depot and get some wood, screws, and the tools you need. When you build it with your hands, you can start to see how it looks and functions in the real world.

Of course, if you're on the more technical end of the spectrum, you may find using a 3D printer more natural for you. There are different ways of prototyping, but what we are aiming at here is a cheap prototype phase. Don't get drawn into the mistake of thinking your first prototype has to be beautiful. It doesn't. The key in this phase is proof of concept and cost-control.

During the crude prototype phase, we're just testing. Does this thing work? Is the functionality effective? You're going to find little tweaks and things you need to change during this stage, so why spend a bunch of money on a prototype you're not going to use?

Another way to prototype is to go to a store, buy a couple of existing products, break them apart, and combine their pieces in a new way. You'll find a lot of products that are created this way. If it's something a little complicated, or you don't feel like you can create it from scratch, you can still create a low-cost prototype just by going out and grabbing things that are already made and were professionally manufactured. In fact, your prototype might look pretty nice that way, because all those things have the aesthetics of professional, market-ready products.

Once you have that first, initial prototype – and this is just for validation purposes, this isn't the prototype we're going to show the world – you then ask yourself a series of questions before you go into the second prototype:

- How big should this be?
- Do I need to make adjustments to the ratios or the color?
- Is this comfortable or will it be uncomfortable?
- Is there a part of this that's too poky?

You'll see what needs to be changed in one second with this prototype in your hands – things you would never see from a drawing.

This second, improved version of your prototype is in between your "only for yourself" prototype and your final one. This is the type of prototype that you'll be able to show to people to get ideas and feedback, but also to potential manufacturers.

After you've gone through the above stages, you can then jump into using 3D printing or hire a CNC machinist to create a perfect prototype. Three-dimensional printing and CNC machining are automated processes that turn your CAD drawings into exact models of what your product will look like when completed.

One thing I want to talk about because it's the elephant in the room is money. We want to control cost, and you may be in a situation where you simply can't afford to spend thousands of dollars in the prototyping stage. You can't afford the cost of an engineer, or to get expensive time on a CNC or a 3D printing machine.

In that case, I'm still there with you. I created the WOW system to help you move your WOW IDEAS forward while spending as little money as possible. One way to save on prototyping is to go to a local engineering college and find a student to work with.

Colleges have amazing students with access to 3D printing. They have amazing tools for the students to work with. I do this all the time; I'll find some engineering students, and they'll help me transition from my rough prototypes into something perfect. They're allowed to use those machines for free, so they have access to tools that would normally be very expensive because it's part of their education process. And it's amazing. They can create prototypes for you for free – you just pay for all the materials. They do all the work and the research. But remember: it's education first. They're learning by doing. There's a great value for them; they get to be part of a real-world product.

You can work with local universities or small business development firms in your town to quickly get things done without spending much money. Just realize that education comes before your timeline, so when working with students, don't expect quick turnaround times.

Another option, which is what I often do now, is establishing relationships with overseas factories, whether in China, Mexico, Thailand, or Vietnam. You can develop that relationship through Skype; you don't even have to fly there in person. There are a lot of times where the factory will also do the prototyping for you. They'll put up the cost and build it in-house because they want to be the factory you use when you go into manufacturing.

This might be a little advanced for first-time inventors, but for some people, this is the perfect fit. You might be thinking, "What happens if someone steals my idea?" We'll talk about protection later, but as you go into the manufacturing phase, you'll see that there are challenges no matter what. If your idea is good, people will try to steal it one way or another.

But when you work with a factory, they'll make a bunch of samples, and they'll even pay for tooling to get your product out there because they believe in it. If you have a WOW IDEA, other people will see it and experience the WOW, and they'll want to be part of it. They'll want to be on that journey with you.

We want to get together the best prototype we can, using the resources and finances we have available, for one reason: we're about to start asking people for money. Whether you're going to ask investors, potential customers via crowdfunding, or whether you're going to show it to a company that may be interested in licensing it from you or simply to friends and family, the prototype is critical to getting into that next stage and getting people excited to invest, pre-order, or license.

Reflection Questions

1. When you've thought about prototyping in the past, what's been your number one hurdle? Has it been cost, time, or lack of technical ability? Are you uncomfortable or unnatural with tools? What's been holding you back?

2. Do you now see a path to manufacturing that works for you, and what is that path? Which of these ways of building your prototype makes you feel the most comfortable? Do you see the value of going to a local university? Which path seems most natural to you, and are you most likely to use?

3. Are you feeling the same excitement as I do when you think about building an actual prototype of your product?

Activity

Whether you already have a prototype or are about to create your first one, make sure you read this book at least one time through. Creating the perfect prototype will be the single most important stage of the Invent WOW process. Get this right, and you increase your chances of success 10x.

1. Your first task is to research and prepare to build your proto-

type. What I want you to do is take each of the different ways of prototyping and find out how they work. With your first idea, head down to Home Depot and look at the parts they have available to see what building a prototype this way would cost. Also, think about your ability with your hands.

2. You're going to go and look at a place that has parts or a couple of other products you could buy, chop up, and cobble together to build a prototype, and see what that would cost.

3. Find where in your town you can get access to a CNC or 3D printing expert and see what that costs. Also, find out about the process of getting the CAD drawings done because you have to have perfect drawings before you commit to an expensive CNC or 3D-printed model.

4. You can even get creative and see as I did, if there are local people whose time is affordable, whether it's a few guys in a metal shop or simply a garage tinker guy, or maybe you know someone who's really good working with wood. Find out what it would cost or the accessibility for this type of person.

Work your way down through each of these steps. You may find that there are several different engineering colleges, postgraduate schools, or trade schools in your area; make a list of them in your notebook with their contact details. You can even reach out and find out about the process. "Hey, I'm a (product developer) inventor, I'm working on a new project, and I'd love to work with some of your engineering students. I'd be happy to provide all the materials and support and bring in an external project."

And if you feel up to it, you could go to the next level and reach out to some factories in China or other countries to learn about their prototyping process.

5

THE NDA

On a frosty Christmas Eve in 1995, instead of spending time with my loved ones, I was ensconced with one of the top infomercial companies in the world. Sitting there trying to hammer out a deal with one of the top TV infomercial producers, I was on the brink of success with the Ab Roller. He was going to license the exclusive TV rights to my device and broadcast it all over television.

There was only one thing that stood between us and a deal – I wanted a one-hundred-thousand-dollar advance. He refused, and the deal collapsed. There were already knockoffs all over TV, so I knew this would be a massive hit. The rip-offs proved my idea was a WOW IDEA.

Even with all the other successful infomercials out there selling knockoffs of my innovation, he was still afraid. He was afraid that the product wouldn't sell, and he refused to take the risk with me. He kept repeating all the reasons he couldn't do it – that he didn't know how big the market was and his fear of the knockoffs out there flooding the market.

His fear kept him from closing the deal with me. No way was I trusting an infomercial company with my device without an upfront show of faith. Within a year, thirty infomercial companies released knockoffs of the Ab Roller. But one company never did.

Infomercial companies clearly weren't afraid of my patent. But at the start of negotiations that frosty holiday season, I did one thing right. I made him sign my nondisclosure agreement. He knew that document was ironclad and I would be able to sue him into oblivion if he joined the party and tried to rip off my product, too.

Most people, when they think about releasing their first invention to the world, think about going down the patent process. We're going to cover patents when it's the correct time to file for a patent, but it's not at this stage in the process.

In the United States, you can start the process by filing a provisional patent application, and from that date, you have one year to transition into the full non-provisional patent. Here's the critical element some inventors are not aware of, and I want to make sure you know this: when you file your full patent application, it's built on top of exactly what you put into your provisional patent application. During that one-year provisional period, you can't change anything.

But we're not finished with our prototyping. We need to go through a few more steps to get our final invention perfect. Until everything is perfect and we are ready to show it to the market, we don't want to jump into the patent game. Patents cost money and reveal information about your product; we want to wait until it's perfect.

In this part of the process, what we really want to do is start to show our invention to friends and family, just as I showed the Ab Roller to people in my office. I wanted to get their feedback; I wanted to see people use it and get their reactions because when people are playing around with it, they'll see things that you didn't see before. They might say, "Oh, if this was padded a little bit." Or, "This works for short people, but I'm taller, and the edge doesn't reach the back of my head."

All we need at this stage is a simple document: a nondisclosure agreement that establishes a couple of critical elements. First of all, they can't reveal anything about you or about the invention. The second thing is that any idea or improvement they come up with is yours. They don't become your co-inventor if they have an idea or give you feedback and you implement it. You do want to have a little bit of protection at this phase, but it doesn't require going to a lawyer yet. I have templates of these documents available as part of my advanced training program on my website, and you can find them at InventWow.com.

The crucial point is that they're not allowed to use your idea or tell anyone about your idea. This way, if they take your idea and release it to the world because they signed an NDA, you have an open-and-shut court case because you don't have to prove they infringed your patent. They have already agreed not to. A patent protects your product using claims that allow you to sue anyone who's stolen your product. This can take years of litigation, but an NDA signed by a specific person or company is an agreement in advance not to share or steal your idea. They have already admitted infringement if they were to run out and copy your idea.

Once you have your first NDA ready, you want to make sure that people sign it before they look at anything. Here's what you need to understand: it's not offensive to ask someone to sign an NDA. It's normal.

The only reason someone would refuse to sign an NDA is if they're considering stealing your idea or if they are a company who already has a line of similar products; they can't sign NDAs for fear that you might sue them.

Most companies like this have their own version of an NDA, which basically states the following: "We may already have thought of your idea, and if so, we will not be bound by the NDA." I can tell you because I've done this many times. I've been on both sides.

An NDA is just a document that says, "I won't steal your idea from you unless I am already working on a similar one." It doesn't provide you with any other powers, and it doesn't create any other legal precedent other than if they steal and try and sell your idea, in which case you can sue them. An NDA is nothing more than a paper handshake that states, "I want to work with you, and I trust you will not steal or copy my idea."

Once you have your document in place, print a few copies, and be professional about how you store your documentation physically or online because this is a critical document you may need in the unlikely event that the person signing it actually copies your idea.

Nondisclosures are a very simple and low-cost way to protect your idea in the early stages. And where you use it most of the time is getting feedback from people. These are the three different types of nondisclosure agreement:

1) **The Feedback NDA.** This is for family, friends, and potential future customers. You just want to get feedback. This is a nice NDA that's binding but friendly. We're basically saying, "I want your feedback; please sign here that you willing to give me feedback." And it's a little less stressful. Instead of handing somebody a nondisclosure agreement that looks like a legal document stating you're going to sue their ass off just for showing them your idea, you want it to be a friendly agreement – but it's still an NDA.

2) **The Work-For-Hire NDA.** This is the document you will use when talking to potential manufacturers. Have them sign this document stating that they can't build your product or anything like it without your express permission. This document covers you in case negotiations fall through.

3) **The Work-For-Hire Agreement.** That's where you're going to hire an engineer, designer or manufacturer – somebody to make a design and help you with your product. And again, they agree that if they improve your product, you get all the rights. With this document, when your manufacturers, your video production, and all the people that you're going to be working with sign some form of an NDA right up front, it protects you from them sharing and telling

other people. With this document, your manufacturer can make your product, but you are still the owner.

❖

Reflection Questions

1. Has anyone in your life ever asked you to sign a nondisclosure agreement, and how did it make you feel? Did you think of it as a big deal?

2. Have you thought about the legal process and how to protect yourself at each phase of your invention process?

3. Have you been relying on your inventor's notebook as a piece of evidence to protect you if someone steals your idea? Do you still think that's the best form of protection?

4. When thinking about asking your friends and family to sign a little document before you show them your invention, how does that make you feel? Are you hesitant, or does it feel like not a big deal? We want to deal with those emotions before we get into that moment.

❖

Protect Yourself Activity

We're going to go into a lot more detail about protecting yourself and patents later on, but for now, your task is to begin researching and understanding the different parts of this process. I recommend that you begin learning about NDAs and put your first NDA together.

As I mentioned earlier, you can go to my website, where I share copies of all the legal documents I use as part of my advanced training programs. But you don't necessarily have to use my documents; you can find boilerplate NDAs online. Based on the information I've given you, and what you need your nondisclosure agreement to include, you can put together what you need.

Again, your activity for this chapter can go in two directions. If your invention's not ready to show anyone, then you can just do the first half of this activity. And that is to get your NDA written and printed. Get it as perfect as you can so that it's ready for showtime.

If your invention is ready to show to people, then you're going to get them to sign these NDAs. Get people in your life to sign the agreements before you show anything.

6

THE FEEDBACK

A critical component of the feedback stage is the pre-patent NDA protection. Once we have that done, it's time to get feedback from real people who are your ideal future customer.

Depending on what stage your prototype is in, people may not be able to actually use it, or they'll just see its functionality, but they can still suggest things you didn't think of, like, "It looks uncomfortable," or, "Why doesn't it have this feature?"

The one danger and caveat for dealing with friends and family is that they're not always going to tell you when your idea stinks or when something isn't right. You have to create an environment where you can say, "Look, I care more about honest feedback than I do about my emotions." And you have to stick to that.

You want to have people see the idea and be absolutely honest with you and not worry about hurting your feelings. If somehow you have gotten to this stage and have an absolute dumb idea, wouldn't you rather your friends and family tell you before you start investing a lot of money in the next stage? It's much better to get honest feedback now when we can still control how much money we've spent. Coming up with ideas is easy, turning them into WOW products takes time, work, and your hard-earned money. Ask for honest feedback.

You might have an absolute WOW IDEA, and people will just go nuts for it. But I can tell you that my Ab Trainer changed during this process. I got feedback from people about a few different things – how to make it fit for short and tall people, how to make it comfortable in different ways, how to put the correct padding on and so on. These are really important steps. As long as each person you're showing your product to signs an NDA, you can get creative with them.

The next phase after you ask friends and family is where you start talking to manufacturers. When you're thinking about the process of getting it made – your conceptual prototype is now done – we're moving into a level of professional feedback. This is where I went and talked to some pipe benders. You talk to people who could manufacture your product, and this could be a factory in China or in your hometown. It's very important, at this point, to have the next iteration, complete with all the changes you learned from the initial feedback stage. But before you begin showing your refined prototype to professionals, you will need a "work for hire agreement."

We're still using an NDA, but this version is more specific about them not being able to release a similar product or compete with you. It's a slightly stronger NDA than the one we use with our friends and family, and it's more specific because it's for someone in the same industry who could quite easily release the product themselves.

Knock-offs are often made at the same factory the main product is. The work-for-hire NDA says, "You aren't allowed to make or sell this unless I have agreed to allow you to do so." And you also want to make sure that your NDA includes that any ideas that come from your relationship with them don't change ownership; they're just part of the work for hire relationship. They are agreeing to share their ideas on how to improve your idea with the understanding that you own their ideas as well; you don't want someone to give you some idea and then claim ten percent of the new version. This can happen, and it's what we're protecting you from here.

You do not want somebody who's experienced in manufacturing or product development to know what your product is without signing an NDA because they are in a strong position where they could put you at risk. During this phase, you're going to have them look at your product and see what they say because they'll know about manufacturing. They may say, "If we change this bit one percent, it'll cut your cost down ten percent." And you want to have that kind of information.

You may find that this is the perfect partner for you and decide to work together. At this point, you bring in your work-for-hire agreement, which simply says that they're making the product for you, and you retain total ownership of it.

When they start making it, they may discover other elements that need to be tweaked and changed to improve the process. And again, the work-for-hire agreement says they're working for you for a flat fee, and there's no chance of them taking ownership.

I know that talking about all these legal documents can be a little overwhelming here; that's why I provide most of that information on my website as well. But it is important to talk about it here because these are the most common pitfalls for inventors. Most inventor horror stories happen at this phase, and they are primarily due to mistakes with the documentation.

At this point, you might decide to have your product licensed out, but we still want to have a production-ready model. The further down the path you can take it, the easier it will be. Shortly, we'll talk about your "show and sell" video and running a crowdfunding campaign. Both of those can dramatically change how much money you'll make when you go down a licensing path, so even if you're not planning on launching it yourself, going through this process is very valuable.

Get all the feedback you can, protect yourself, and you can have an amazing product ready to go into the money phase, which is coming in the next section.

❖

Reflection Questions

1. Do you know any inventors, or have you had an experience in the past, where a legal mistake cost you or someone a great deal of money?

2. How do you feel about all this legal mumbo-jumbo? Does it make you a little uncomfortable, or can you see how having a simple series of documents helps you have yourself covered? Does that help you feel a little bit more comfortable now you have a template to go with, rather than trying to have to figure it out?

3. When thinking about your idea and manufacturing it, which parts of the process make you the most nervous? Dial into where you feel a little bit overwhelmed so that you know and have prepared yourself for that phase.

4. What's your plan for dealing with the legal aspects of your business? Do you have a lawyer in place? Have you figured out what you're going to do? Are you just planning on buying some legal documents from a website? Do you still feel comfortable with that plan? Or maybe you have no plan at all and are just realizing you need to implement a plan?

Activity

Now that you understand the pre-patent protection process, using NDAs, and work for hire agreements, you can start showing your product to people and get real-world feedback. You'll notice, sometimes, that people are hesitant to give you feedback, or you might even create an environment where you are so enthusiastic that they don't want to hurt your enthusiasm.

As you start showing your product, your goal is to observe yourself and see if you're creating a problem. If you're so enthusiastic that everyone says, "This is the greatest product ever," and they don't point out anything about it, there's the one percent chance that you're the smartest person in the world, and your invention is perfect without getting any external feedback, or far more likely, people are uncomfortable telling you what they don't like, or they don't want to burst your bubble. That can affect your business in a very negative way.

Practice your process of sharing products. In fact, I would recommend that you watch a lot of those television shows where people pitch their product in different ways. I want you to see good and bad pitches and see how people seeking feedback do it right and do it wrong.

Once you've finished getting the feedback from your friends and family, go into the feedback stage with possible manufacturers. And when you find that right manufacturer, start working on that relationship. See what it will cost to get your device made. You might not be ready to place an order at that stage; this is very normal. But even if you don't have the funding to place an order right away, you still need to know what it will cost to determine the selling price, profit margin, and if people are even willing to buy it.

We're going to cover that a lot more in the next section, but this is research into manufacturing that you're going to have to do. I recommend comparing prices between different countries. It's much cheaper to manufacture in China, and that's why most people do that, but of course, there can be quality control challenges if it's your first time.

If you can't go to the factory in person to observe the product and the manufacturing, you could end up with a shipping crate of something that's not quite what you expected. You do want to be very frosty in the manufacturing phase. Make sure they send you sample units. This is the time where you're going to experiment, get samples built and find how you're going to manufacture it, and you want to get to the point where you have a final version that's not just a prototype – you want a working, usable version that is ready for your customer to buy.

7

THE PATENT

Understanding protection is critical. You're at the point where you've finalized your prototype. You've gone through the entire process, and now you have something that people are chomping at the bit and ready to buy. You had everybody sign NDAs. Now we want to go to the next level of protection.

When you're going to disclose your product to the public, the law is very specific: you have to file at least a provisional patent application. The law in the United States establishes that you have one year to file a patent from the day you share it with the public. But the rule also states that the first person to file is the owner.

If you launch a crowdfunding campaign, someone can see your product and file for it if you haven't. Before you launch that crowdfunding campaign or any pre-test, you'll want to file a provisional patent application to lock in your date of conception.

Up to this point, you've used NDAs, work-for-hire NDAs, nondisclosure, and non-compete agreements. Since the product has not been publicly disclosed, you're protected. This gives you more time, because with a good product, you may spend months or even a year refining and perfecting it. And that's why I like to use an NDA before I jump into going for a patent – we need that extra time.

Before you publicly expose your invention, you're going to file a provisional patent application. It's not a full patent, but it locks in the date of conception. Filing this with the government is going to cost you between $250 and $1500, and because we're trying to cost-control as part of the Invent WOW process, we wait until that critical moment. We file for a patent only when we are sure that our idea is great. We don't want to file a patent for an idea that we're not going to take to market.

When you file this provisional patent, it gives you a year to transition and pay the higher fee for a full patent. The cost of the full patent varies based on whether you do it yourself, with a lawyer, or get a patent expert to help you write out the description.

You can file a provisional patent yourself by going to the USPTO (the United States Patent and Trademark Office) website; grab that provisional application, fill it out, and upload it. When they send back a confirmation, you have your date locked in, and you do not want to forget this date; you now have twelve months before you have to apply for the full patent. The date you file the provisional patent is now legally your invention date.

Having a provisional patent discourages other companies from trying to rip you off. It becomes more financially sound for them to do a deal with you rather than steal your product. If you have a great idea, people are going to want to steal it. People are going to want to make as much money as they can. I've been down that road, and I want to protect you from it. Even though it's only a provisional patent and it's only for twelve months, for just two or three hundred dollars, it will protect you from a lot of potential heartache, and it will open the door to great licensing deals.

It's important to note that a provisional patent is not any protection on its own. If you fail to convert it into a full patent, then it's meaningless. All the provisional patent does is provide you with a twelve-month window to file for a real patent. You can't sue anyone with a provisional patent. It simply locks down your date as the "first to file."

When you're designing your provisional patent, the way you

design it is critical because when you request a full patent a year later, you can only make the same claims as on your provisional document.

When I'm designing and filing a patent application, I want to do two things: I want to file for all the features and how my product works, and I also want my patent to include every knock-off. Look at your product, and think, "If I wanted to rip this person off and steal this invention, how would I modify it just enough to squeak past their patent?" If your patent is very specific and only covers the exact design and shape of your product, then someone could make minor modifications and create a version that is functionally identical but outside your patent.

Your patent is everything; it's permission to sue. A patent won't stop people from stealing your idea, but when they do, you can go after them. By describing all the different variations of knock-offs, you can widen your patent and expand your protection. Take all the time you need to design your patent, whether you're doing it yourself or bringing in expert help. If you can afford it, this is a good moment to spend a little bit of money.

Patent attorneys are very good at helping to design the correct language and correctly describing your product, but they're not so good at thinking of how someone will knock it off, and how you need to widen the scope of your patent. This part requires the inventor mind more than it requires the legal mind, and I want you to be aware of that as you go through this process; a mistake in the patent can destroy your business.

The next question I get asked quite often is, "Should I wait the full twelve months to transition my full patent into a patent application?" Getting a patent issued takes a long time, so the sooner you file that full patent, the sooner you get that level of protection.

If you have a great WOW IDEA, you throw it on a crowdfunding campaign and suddenly blast through your goal in the first couple of hours, do not wait to file your patent. You immediately want to file the strongest patent you can get, and as you have raised funds so quickly, you can afford a really solid patent attorney. There are loads of sketchy companies that just watch crowdfunding campaigns to see anything that's a hit and make a knock-off, so the sooner you go from provisional to full protection, the better.

You don't just want to go to any patent attorney. There is a very different process for defending something like an Ab Roller versus defending something like a new version of a smoke alarm. Technology products are different from software products and mechanical products. All the different types of patents and products are litigated in different ways based on the specific category, so you want a firm that connects with your type of invention because they'll understand more of the nuances.

When you're writing a patent, the claims are everything. And I want to stress again that the inventor plays a critical role in describing how the invention works, what makes it unique, and how to include all the different possible ways that this product could be knocked off, so that the patent attorney can take those tidbits of valuable information and turn them into patent language that a judge who's in the middle of litigation can instantly understand. It's a partnership process between you and your patent firm, and it's preparing yourself just in case that litigation happens.

Throughout this entire process, I've tried to show you how to bootstrap and cost-control as much as possible. But the patent is the fulcrum upon which your entire business will pivot, and a lot of inventors make a mistake here and decide they can't afford a patent.

I've seen this happen to young inventors, and it breaks my heart when they spend a great deal of money going through the prototyping phase, and when it's time for the patent, the budget's not there, so they end up filing a patent on the cheap using patent software.

All it takes is for a tiny little mistranslation to slip through the cracks. Patent software just translates regular talk into patent talk, and we have all seen those funny videos on YouTube where someone takes a song lyric, translates the song into another language using translating software, then translates it back, and it looks nothing like the original. One tiny mistake in a patent can ruin you. All it takes is one wrong letter and believe me, you'll be wishing you'd paid a little bit more for a good attorney.

There are some online platforms that have changed our approach to legal documents. Instead of having to pay a lawyer for every single legal template, we're now used to going to these websites and paying a lower price for boilerplate templates. The problem is that what you're doing is unique. For certain areas of your business, if you're filing an LLC or incorporating, it's fine to use those templates, but your patent is critical because it's your whole business. You can have the greatest invention in the world, but if your patent doesn't match your invention, you don't own it.

I've talked about some of the other documents that I make available on my website: the nondisclosure agreement, the work-for-hire agreement, and the feedback agreements. You can find them online for free, but the reason why I sell them as part of my more advanced training course is that I paid an attorney $5,000 to go through my versions and make sure they perfectly matched the Invent WOW process. I want you to notice that in no way, shape, or form do I offer anything along the way of a patent template or a patent application template. You have to hire the right person for that so that your patent is perfect.

It takes one to two years for a patent to get issued. The process is getting faster, but if you've ever dealt with the IRS, you know that the federal government is not about doing things fast. It moves very slowly, and two years can be a long time to watch other people making millions while knocking off your product.

However, you can speed things up with a "petition to make special," and if you have people knocking you off like crazy, and they're causing irreversible harm, then the patent office will accelerate the process for you. Of course, you do have to pay an additional fee, but you'll get your patent in six to nine months.

There are several different types of patents, and your attorney will walk you through the right type you need but let me just mention each of these different types of patent, so as you're looking at it, and you're choosing a patent attorney, you make sure you go for the right kind.

The first type of patent is a utility patent; this is about the function, or how the device works. Then there is the design patent, which is an ornamental appearance patent. I often see people with a design patent who think they're protected, but someone can take your device and slightly tweak how it looks or change the shape just enough to get outside your patent description, and they're not infringing.

A design patent doesn't offer much protection because people aren't buying your device for how it looks; it is the weakest form of protection. Other patents include method patents, software patents, chemical patents, and plant patents, which include things like making hybrid plants. If you're more of a botanist inventor, these other types of patents might apply to you.

Make sure you file for a provisional patent before you run any tests or crowdfunding campaigns.

Reflection Questions

1. When thinking about launching your invention and cost-controlling, does it now make sense why we limited your spending as much as possible to get to this point?

2. When looking back at the plans we've been drawing up, and looking at what it would cost to prototype, do you need to shift some money around and maybe go for a cheaper prototyping process, so you have more funds available to get the right type of patent?

3. How would you feel if you had an amazing invention, you filed the patent on your own for $100, and then someone made a non-functioning knock-off and made $10 million, and you couldn't even sue them?

4. Think about the future and think about your invention. We get so caught up in the emotional moment, and it's very tempting to only think about how excited we are about our invention. Do you under-

stand why the strategic thinking element (thinking about knock-offs and other ways to develop your product) has been included throughout the entire Invent WOW process? Is it starting to connect together?

❖

Activity

As much as inventors are creative types, and we hate thinking about patents and lawyers, this is probably the most important chapter in the book when it comes to your income streams. We're going to try a couple of really cool activities, and the more of these activities you do, the better.

Let's go through each exercise together.

1. Find a product on Amazon that has a knock-off version on AliBaba.com or AliExpress.com. Look at the two different versions of the product and see if the knock-off is different enough. Then, go through Google Patents and try to find the patent for that original product.

You can see the patent that the person filed, and you can ask yourself, "Is this Chinese company infringing or not? Did this person make a mistake with their patent? And is that why they're open to knock-offs?" This activity is very useful because you get to go through what I've been through without the emotion, the pain, and the tears.

2. Find an interesting product that is similar to your invention. Find a device that has recently been in an infomercial or a crowdfunding campaign or just a new device that is doing really well on Amazon.

Your job is to create a knock-off version. We're going to do this in two steps. First, look at it and say, "How can I make something a little bit different that's just different enough that I could get around their patent?"

Then, as part of the same exercise, you're going to try and find their patent through Google Patents or the USPTO office and see if your idea would squiggle around their patent without infringing. If your idea infringes, try again and see if you can find a way around their patent.

The aim of this activity is to teach you how to think strategically to protect yourself from this happening to you. The more you get into this mindset, the more you develop this skill of getting around patents, the better you'll get at describing your own patents and protecting yourself.

3. Work on widening your claims. You already have a small army of people who have already signed an NDA with you, so thinking outside the box can be very helpful. What I like to do is ask those people, "How would you knock this off?" You can ask your manufacturer as well, "If you were trying to get around this patent, what would you do?"

Remember: the manufacturer is going to be manufacturing for you – they don't want somebody getting around your patent because they lose money too. They're on your side now. Your friends who've signed an NDA will have ideas too, and they might see it in a different way. I do recommend utilizing people who have already signed NDAs with you for some extra help.

4. Your final task is to prepare and put together an entire application for your provisional patent and find the right attorney within your part of the market, so you can go ahead and file your provisional patent.

I've shared as much information with you as I possibly can about this process, but if you have other questions, my email address is at the beginning and the end of this book. I love helping up-and-coming inventors throughout this process, and I know this part can be a little bit daunting. That's why we're on a cooperative venture together.

Work your way through these activities as far as is appropriate for where you are, start to sharpen your skills at creating knock-offs, and then I'll see you in the next chapter.

8

THE TRADEMARK

Most inventors spend so much time thinking about patents that they forget all about trademarks, and I certainly don't want that to happen to you. Once you've locked in your branding, protecting that name is critical. Copyright law in America is constantly shifting, thanks to Mickey Mouse. As the law stands now, a patent will only last twenty, but your trademarks will outlive you.

The first Copyright Act in the United States was passed in 1790 and only provided fourteen years of protection with the option to renew for an additional fourteen years if you were still alive. The law was modified a few times, and by the early 1900s, the length had doubled, and you could file for twenty-eight years of protection and renew for an additional twenty-eight years.

This was the state of the world when Disney released a little cartoon called Steamboat Willy in 1928. The last thing Disney wants is for that cute little mouse to enter the public domain, so every time their protection is about to expire, Disney lobbies Washington, DC to change the law again. They have pushed for multiple changes, and this is a very good thing for us. As it stands right now, Mickey will fall into the public domain in 2023, but I have a pretty strong feeling that we can expect a new Copyright Act to appear in Congress before then.

Before we dig into trademarks, I want to make sure you're absolutely clear. Even though these laws are called "Copyright Acts," they are protecting ideas and names, not inventions. This applies to inventors because the way we name our products is critical. There is a reason we discussed branding before testing, launching, or licensing.

We have covered the process of getting a patent in great detail in the last chapter, but that's not the end of our journey. Patents can be very good, but also very limiting.

A patent in the United States only lasts twenty years. But a trademark can last for one hundred years. I own the trademark on Ab Roller for fitness equipment, and it will be here when I am long gone.

You can make a fitness device that looks just like mine or any other fitness product when that patent runs out, but you cannot call it an Ab Roller; I own that name. When you have a great name, the trademark can be even more valuable than the product. And in fact, multiple products can be built around the same name. If your first idea is not WOW enough, but you have a great name, you can use it for the next invention as well.

There are some great names out there that just stick in your mind and are stronger than the product itself. These names demand a very high price even after the patents run out. Frisbee is one of my favorite trademarks to talk about. The Frisbee started off as a simple pie plate from the Frisbee pie factory. Now the name is ubiquitous with flying disks, and the trademark keeps them in business, despite the fact that the patent has expired.

Your invention can easily outlive your patent because twenty years isn't really that long. You can have your great WOW IDEA explode when you're twenty, and when you're forty, the money dries up. The patent's gone. But the trademark is better and more powerful.

Trademarks are much easier to defend than patents. With a patent court case, it's all about opinions and determinants and seeing how similar the device is to your original invention, or if they made just enough tweaks to make it seem different.

With a trademark, it is much simpler. If you're using my name, you're using a term that I own, and I can send you a notice to stop. There are certain companies that are experts at this. If you want to see trademarks in action, make a website with the word "LinkedIn" in the title. They're one of the fastest companies in the world at finding you and taking control of that domain. You can make a website called "ilovelinkedin.com," and it can be all about how it's your favorite platform and you recommend everyone use it, and they'll take it away from you within days.

Another great example is the word "Jedi." George Lucas and his company don't even own a trademark on the word "Jedi." They trademarked the word "Jedi Knight," but see what happens if you use the word "Jedi" without his permission.

Even if your blog is all about how brilliant Jedis are and how you love Star Wars, if your website ever started making money, they would take it away because he owns a term that he invented. The word "Jedi" did not exist before the movie Star Wars. The way you name and brand your product is critical because if you create a trademark that becomes well-known, like my Ab Roller, then you could very well have created a golden goose.

What's in a Name?

Powerful names stay with us, and brand names can become more dominant than what they represent. When's the last time you asked for a facial tissue? Did you call it a Kleenex, which is a brand name? Do you call it table tennis, or do you use the brand name Ping Pong? Do you call it a flying disc or a Frisbee?

When naming your product, it's worth spending as much time as needed on it. When I'm naming a product, I go through a three-step process.

Step one: try and relate the name to the dramatic difference of your WOW IDEA. Let's look at the dramatic difference of my Ab

Coaster: the WOW difference is the pair of curved steel rails that resemble roller coaster tracks.

Step two: use a word that literally describes what the product does and/or include words that rhyme or sound the same, like in Coca-Cola, which happens to be one of the most memorable trademarks in the world. The original formula was made from Coca leaves and Kola Nut. The name rhymes and sounds the same, with the alliteration of the "co" sound.

Step three: make it fun if possible; to most people, roller coasters are fun.

The goal of a great trademark is to create a name that so anyone who hears it instantly knows what you're talking about. Just like someone should instantly be able to understand exactly what your invention does the second they see it; a good name should have the same effect.

I've seen weak inventions with a great name sell for a very high price. It's fine to go through multiple product names as well. I transitioned the name of my product from the Ab Trainer to the Ab Roller because Ab Roller was the top brand on TV, and I was able to take control of the name as part of my settlements.

The Process of Trademarking

Before you commit to your name, make sure it's not descriptive, like my Ab Trainer. It is very hard to obtain a registered trademark on a descriptive name. However, you can still use the name, and if you're lucky like I was, and over time that name is used over and over in the public domain to identify your WOW product, then you can go back to the USPTO and apply for a trademark again. That's what I did, and it was granted. I was able to prove that my trade name had acquired the necessary distinctiveness of a trademark.

It's always a good idea to come up with non-descriptive names like Ab Roller, Ab Coaster, etc., which are not as descriptive as Ab Trainer.

Some of the best trademarks out there are metaphors and have no obvious link to the product, but once you understand the story behind the brand, you gain a real attachment to the brand name.

A good example is Apple. The Apple logo is "knowledge" bitten out of the "apple." A great metaphor allows you to join in the activity of the word. Apple's browser, Safari, is a perfect example, or Google, which is the word "googol" misspelled. Googol means the number 1 plus 100 zeros or an unlimited number, which plays on what you can search for on the Internet using Google.

Before you file for a trademark, search on Google and the patent website to make sure nobody else is already using it in your category. The USPTO has a great section where you can search and type in the name of your product to see if anyone else is using it, and it's the exact same search that lawyers will charge you hundreds or even thousands of dollars to perform.

Once you've confirmed that the name is available to the best of your knowledge, you can file for your trademark. There are loads of lawyers who will tell you that you need to spend thousands of dollars on the research and application process, but you really don't. There is a series of videos walking you through the entire trademark process directly on the USPTO site, and the whole process will take you a few hours at most.

Once you've filed for a trademark, your inbox will explode with emails from lawyers informing you that most trademarks aren't approved and that you need to hire them to fix your filing. What those lawyers don't bother to tell you is that most of those failed applications are approved after a few minor alterations. The trademark approval process usually takes around six months, and if you aren't approved on the first try, don't sweat it.

Call the phone number in your notification email, and someone from USPTO will walk you through what you need to change to get approved. It's a surprisingly painless process.

Once your trademark is approved, you are in great shape! You now own the name of your invention or company. After using that name for five years, you can file an additional application to make your trademark non-contestable. This takes your protection to the next level and means that nobody can even try to come after your name. It's now written in stone.

Reflection Questions

1. When thinking about the name for your product, would someone immediately know what your product is, what it does, and how it works from the name?

2. Do you want to be more like Twitter or more like Facebook? Do you want a title or a name that people easily and instantly understand? Are you trying to create a brand-new word that forces education?

3. Spelling is critical. How are you planning on spelling your product name? Think of Dribbble, one of the most popular platforms used by designers and photographers to self-promote and network. It was very easy to trademark the three-B version of the word because it's not a real word; it's a way to use a common word and become unique. Think about these businesses and products where the name is very clear, and businesses and names where you only know what it is if you've learned and been educated about the product.

4. One of my friends has a product called the Copper Chef, a two-word title. Do you know what that product is? Does it stick in your head? It's making millions, and it's very easy from the title to know what it is. Do you see the value in having a name this simple?

5. Sit down and brainstorm multiple ideas and names for your product. Ask your friends and get external opinions. Be willing to pivot if you discover other people don't understand what your product name is.

Activity

1. Your first task is a research activity. Go online and look at prod-

ucts in your category that are similar to your WOW invention. Notice how they're named. What is their naming convention? Check when the products are doing well; how are they named? Are you in a category where most products have one-word names, two-word names, or three-word names? Long, descriptive names can actually damage a product.

I worked with someone recently who was adamant about having a long, descriptive title. But it was a nine-word title. You know what happens when you have a nine-word product? People make their own nickname for it. They shorten the name how they want to, not how you want to, so you lose an element of control of your own product.

Research and find names that are clear and powerful. Brainstorm what kind of names work well for products in your category. Just remember that sometimes, a product becomes so ubiquitous that we know the name, even though it originally meant nothing – Kleenex and Frisbee out of context have no meaning; we wouldn't know what they are if we didn't know the product.

2. Create a list of names for some of the potential products you're working on. If you're still thinking about five or ten different products, create name lists for each of them. Brainstorm and get creative, and keep a notebook filled with different name ideas. I can't tell you how valuable it is to have a whole list of names in your notebook that you can change and look at over time.

3. Test your name idea. If you have your product done and you're working on bringing it to market, and you're testing the idea and are ready to sell it, this is a great time to test the name. When you're testing the product design, getting people's feedback throughout this entire process, you could be telling them different names. You could show them a list of product names and say, "Which name matches this item?"

4. Register your trademark. If you're selling your product, if you're launching a crowdfunding campaign, the first $250 should be earmarked for ensuring that you own your name. This can assure

that you drive revenue and make money, even after your twenty-year patent runs out.

If you have a great invention, and the name becomes a household name, the trademark will outlive and be more profitable than the patent itself, even though the trademark is so much easier to capture. If you run into a problem with your trademark application, call that number when they email you before you speak to a lawyer, and just talk to them on the phone; you may find out it's not that big of a deal after all.

PART III

STEP THREE - MONETIZATION

9

THE BRANDING

One day, I received a call from an inventor in Texas named Rob Nelson. He said he had an idea for an ab product where you pulled your legs up while kneeling on a pad that was attached to a set of rails. He called it Ab Razor. I was intrigued, and he sent me a photo. He had made a rough prototype, and I asked him to send me a video. You held on to the top and pulled the pad up the rails. My response was, "This is a really cool motion for training your abs, but your invention is too similar to other things already on the market." But as I was watching his video, I had an "aha" moment. I remembered reading an article in *Men's Health* about rock-hard abs. Abs are really my area of specialty, so I was curious about this article "Hard Abs Made Easy." It showed a picture of a guy hanging from a bar, pulling his legs straight up in the air. This is one of the hardest exercises ever. Sure, if you can do it, your abs will be rock-hard. But just about nobody can do it.

I realized that the bottom-up leg lifts were a big problem for unfit people. That's when I applied the same logic from my Ab Roller. I told Rob to bend the rails and make the seat swivel. He went back to work and delivered exactly what I needed. That was the start of what is now known as the Ab Coaster. As you can see, Rob's idea was a great idea – working your abs from the bottom up. The article in *Men's Health* confirmed the problem. Taking Rob's initial innovation and tweaking it with a curved track turned it into the success it is today.

The name Ab Razor was fun and related to cut abs, but it was not the perfect name Ab Coaster became. The final prototype looked like a little rollercoaster because of the curved track, and we knew that people could relate to the idea. Going to an amusement park or even being on a rollercoaster is fun for most people, and the branding of the Ab Coaster took advantage of all that goodwill. Who wouldn't want the fun of a rollercoaster and the benefit of killer abs?

The branding turned abs exercises, which most people hate, into something fun and enjoyable. Taking a hard exercise and making it fun was an absolute hit. The Ab Coaster has sold over $100,000,000, and it's still selling today.

It's a powerful brand name. It's linked to the uniqueness or the dramatic difference of that product from any other ab product. Once you have created your product, it's time to name it and finalize the design. You want something that is instantly understood by the future customer who is going to buy it.

It's so important that the product is named and designed with your target customer in mind. There is nothing sadder than an amazing product sitting on the shelf of a store because people don't understand it. It's tempting to be clever when naming your product, but if you are too clever, many people simply won't get it.

Imagine that a potential customer is walking down the aisle at the hardware store, grocery store, pharmacy, or wherever your product will be sold. Does the name of the product make it clear exactly what it does? Does it convey the emotion you want to get across?

When naming your product, start with the idea of functionality. Your first name might be "ab trainer that doesn't put stress on your neck." That's a name that makes it clear what the product does. It's not exciting, but it's our starting point. From there, we can start to brainstorm. Add in benefits and descriptive words. What emotions do you want the customer to feel when they see the item? Anything you can do to make something hard appear fun or easy will convert your branding into a win.

When choosing colors, what emotions do you want to convey? There are loads of websites explaining how people react to each color of the rainbow. For example, red conveys anger, embarrassment, passion, and lust. If you want to convey one of those emotions, make your product red. If you want something friendly, go with green. I'm not totally locked into the psychology of colors, but it can be a helpful starting point.

You can also think about where in the house your product will live. Will it live in the living room, the office, the garage, or the kitchen? What colors do people expect in those rooms? Is your item for men or women? I colored my original Ab Roller to match the colors of the other products in the NordicTrack line because that was the one customer I was trying to sell to.

Reflection Questions
1. Who is your ideal customer?
2. Where in the house will your product live?
3. What colors and design features does your ideal customer expect from products living in that room of their house, office, or car?
4. What similar products does yours align with? What are the key design, color, and aesthetic features?

Activity
1. Brainstorm ten names for your product, starting with the most descriptive and ranging to the most fun or exotic. Create a list of your favorite choices and begin to survey people. You can create an online survey and ask your social media friends to guess what the product

does based on its name, or which product name most intrigues them. You can easily market-test the product name without investing any money.

2. Create several variations of your product in different colors. You can do this with drawings and sketches. It only takes a few minutes to change the colors of a digital drawing. Create another online survey with the color options and have people select which version they like the most or would most likely buy. To improve the quality of your results, ask demographic questions as well. Then you can weigh the results based on the respondents being a part of your target customer group.

10

THE TEST

Recently, a friend of mine came to me with an idea for a fitness product to train your abs. Since I've been creating ab fitness products for over twenty years, he wanted to work on it with me. Abs are my wheelhouse, and I was excited to see his invention.

He started with the seed of an idea. Performing a plank is extremely boring. You are just stuck there in the push-up position, holding still for as long as you can. It's an exercise where you literally don't move, and nothing is more boring than holding still while you count the time.

I took his idea and ran with it. Together, we created the Stealth Core Trainer. We had a perfect prototype and gave it the name "stealth" because it's a sneaky, fun way to do plank exercises without realizing how hard you're working out.

We had a product with a name we loved that we were very excited about launching, but before we dumped $100,000 into tooling, we wanted to confirm that other people liked our idea too. We decided to test it using Kickstarter to be sure that people would buy it.

We told our story in the video on Kickstarter and hit our goal of $20,000 in pre-orders on the first day. Over the course of the sixty-day campaign, we raised just under $400,000. At the end of the campaign, we had a lot of pre-orders and more cash than we needed.

Completing your prototyping phase and getting to a product you are ready to share with the world is awesome. You've made it far down the path, and now you are ready to perform a test of your own. At this point, it's tempting to jump right into the production of your WOW IDEA, but please do not skip the testing phase.

You now have a working model of your WOW IDEA. It should resemble what your WOW product will look like if it were listed for sale on Amazon. It's not mandatory that it works perfectly, but it is mandatory that it will work when in production. But before you wire the funds to your manufacturer and order 10,000 pieces, we need to take a few steps to make sure your future customers really want to buy your WOW IDEA.

If you truly want to succeed in the invention world, you have to create products that people want to buy, not what you think they want to buy. The only way to find out if you are on the right track is to test, test, test – true validation is when a person is ready and willing to hand over their hard-earned cash to purchase your WOW gizmo.

Now that you are going to start showing your product to people outside your circle of friends and potential business partners, using nondisclosure agreements is no longer feasible. This is the point in your process where you want to apply for a provisional patent. I will cover the ins and outs of this process in the next section.

Before you launch or license your product, you should run this critical test using Facebook ads and a one-page website or landing page. You create a simple Facebook ad with a picture of your WOW invention, and when people click on that ad, they go to the website that has an "order now" button at the bottom.

You can spend about $100 running ads for the right keywords for your type of product, to see if anyone clicks the "order now" button. You don't even have to be ready to take orders, and you don't need to take any credit card information. This very simple test will let you know if there's any level of interest.

Facebook allows you to target people in an infinite number of ways. For example, let's say your WOW product is a yoga mat. You can create a Facebook audience for women ages 30-60 who are interested or already participate in yoga. This way, your ad will only appear on the Facebook pages of your ideal customers.

Before you start your first ad campaign, let me cover what you want on your website. Because you're just making a one-page website, you can use a simple, free blogging platform like WordPress. All you need is some great pictures of the product, the list of features and benefits, and a button giving people a chance to order.

The features include all the things the product can do and the benefits and tell the customer how your new WOW IDEA will change their lives. For example, when I'm creating a message for an ab product, I can say, "This is a product that helps you get strong abs without causing back pain," where "without pain" starts introducing the benefits as well.

You can create a strong features and benefits list by simply asking yourself the question, "So what?" to describe everything your product will do for the customer. You don't need to spend massive amounts of money hiring copywriters; you can start doing it yourself during this testing phase.

Perhaps you have a device that helps people find their keys when they lose them. In that case, you could say, "The product keeps you from losing your keys." So what? "Never be late for a meeting again." So what? "Don't lose your job." So what? "Don't miss that dream interview to get the job you want to make the money you deserve to support your family." As you experiment with this, you can create two different versions of your website to tweak the test, so that when you transition into full launch, you have more accurate data.

When visitors see your Facebook ad and click on it, they will be redirected onto your one-page website or a landing page. The goal of this page is twofold. First, you want to see if they are interested in pre-ordering your amazing new yoga product. This is where your images and/or video have to do all the selling.

It is important that your product is truly a WOW IDEA – not just a minor improvement on an existing product. It must have features and benefits that are so remarkable that your potential new customer is willing to click the "pre-order now" button. Remember: you don't have any product yet. The goal here is just to validate your idea to see if people are even interested.

Your offer has to be a special price for pre-orders only. Once they click on the "pre-order now" button, they will be asked to enter their name and email. Then a "Thank You" page will appear saying, "You are now on our pre-order list, and we have reserved one (your product name) yoga mat at the special price of only (your discounted price). As soon as our inventory arrives, we will email you for your payment information. Thank you."

This simple test will save you a lot of money, and here's why. You will not have to pay for expensive tooling and order a truckload of product until you are absolutely sure who your ideal customer is and you know they are willing to buy your WOW IDEA. By creating a pre-sale website, you can test different audiences, ads, prices, etc. and capture emails way before you commit to your manufacturer.

Think of it this way: imagine you are having a barbecue at your home, and you invite everyone in the neighborhood. You decide to have burgers and hot dogs. Everyone shows up, and they are all vegetarians. You wasted all that food because you never thought to ask what type of food they wanted.

Now imagine if you sent out an email to all your neighbors and asked them to pick their favorite food off a list. You would have known that ninety percent wanted veggie burgers. I know this sounds simple, but if you are serious about making money with your WOW IDEAS, you need to only focus on products that people want, not what you think they want.

This pre-test comes before crowdfunding and manufacturing. It allows you to save money and find out if people are interested and willing to buy the product in its current form, or if you need to make some alterations. You may need to change the color of the device, the name, the description, or improve the sales message. This is low-cost during the pre-test phase, while it gets much more expensive if you need to make alterations later.

When launching a crowdfunding campaign, which we will discuss in the chapter on launching, it is important that your messaging be direct and clear. It's hard to change messaging in the middle of a crowdfunding campaign, so you want to master your message before that. We know you have a great product; now we want to be sure that when people see it, they get it and want to buy it.

This test also allows you to price-test, so you can find the most profitable price that your customers are willing to pay; you definitely don't want your crowdfunding campaign and e-commerce store to fail because you're not charging enough. You deserve to make as much money as you can, so during the testing phase, be willing to raise the price and see if you get more clicks. We want to find that perfect price number before we launch our campaign.

During the testing phase, what I like to do is to simply say, "This retail price will be X, but only for a few days, you can pre-order my brand-new product for Y, at a massive discount." When you call it a pre-order, it allows you to take an order without having the product ready, and it also gives you time for production and to transfer into a crowdfunding campaign or to negotiate for a higher royalty if you decide to license your product.

Reflection Questions

1. Do you understand the value in testing your ideas before rolling it out?
2. Have you ever seen a product on TV (e.g., a new Coke) that never really hit the market? It still amazes me how these billion-dollar brands waste so much money trying to force new products to the masses without even testing first.
3. Do you understand the power of Facebook marketing?
4. Who is your target market? Do you see the importance of defining exactly who your future customer is?

Activity

1. Create a customer avatar. In other words, describe your ideal customer in as much detail as possible. For example, for the yoga mat, "Carrie is thirty-five years old, has two kids, and is a stay-at-home mom. Her favorite me time is her yoga class. She arrives ten minutes early with her yoga mat to pick her favorite spot in the class. She rolls out her mat, grabs a few yoga blocks, and does a few stretches while chatting with others on either side of her." By writing a simple description of your ideal customer, you will begin the process of knowing exactly what to write and say in your video, copy on your one-page site, etc. You will also know exactly who to target on Facebook.

2. Do an image search for Facebook ads so you can see what they look like; this will give you an idea of exactly how to create your ad.

3. Find a person (or if you are tech-savvy, you can do it yourself) to create a one-page website using WordPress, Shopify, or Squarespace.

4. Take a few photos, create a short video, and begin building your one-page site.

11

THE LICENSE

Sometimes, there simply aren't enough hours in the day to do everything you want. Whether you are a serial inventor or just want to focus on a single part of the market, licensing can be a great option. With the successful prototyping and branding of the Ab Coaster, I decided to license the product to the consumer market. I licensed the rights to the same company that partnered with me with the Ab Roller, Tristar Products.

They licensed the rights to the whole market for the Ab Coaster and produced several infomercials, costing over $300,000 each. We agreed on a licensed royalty, and they sold over $100,000,000 worth of Ab Coasters to the whole market on TV.

I decided to keep the commercial market and launch my own business to health clubs and fitness specialty stores across the country, and to this day, the company still exists. That company sells my Ab Coaster to health clubs all over the world. So that's an example of both business models. I licensed the whole market to a TV infomercial company, who sells it directly to the consumer in the household and to mass retailers such as Walmart and Target. But I kept the commercial business and launched my own company, where we sell commercially to corporations, health clubs, fitness spas, trainers, and high-end home users.

If you want to make money without having to put in a lot of work, licensing might be the right choice for you. You just get to create products, hand them over to another company, and cash a royalty check every ninety days. You don't have to deal with manufacturing, staffing, sales, and marketing. You get to focus just on product creation.

Everyone has a different area of expertise. You may be great at inventing products and don't ever want to run a business – you just want passive income streams. And that's exactly what licensing provides. You go to sleep, you wake up with more money, and you didn't even have to do anything.

If you have good intellectual property, you can patent the product, license it to a good contact (a company that's already got their expertise in that field), and they will send you royalty after royalty. I did that with the Ab Roller, and I've received royalties for many years.

The Process

If you decide to license your product, you need to go through a series of steps to get everything in place. The first step is to find every single company that has a product line your WOW product would fit in with. Do a detailed search and see what they have going on in news articles and on LinkedIn. The more you know about them, the more prepared you are when you message them.

This is your business we're talking about, and you can do it the lazy way, which is where you just email the contact email address for their home website, or you can use LinkedIn and find the person in charge of new products or product acquisition. Rather than having to go through three layers until you reach someone who's a decision-maker, you can get straight to them by being strategic with how you approach each company.

Once you've found the person you want to target, learn about them. Just spend ten or fifteen minutes learning about this person. Have they won any awards? Have they been in any articles, written any articles, or spoken at any conferences?

We're looking for something enough to justify our message or to start our message with a compliment or something nice. "I saw that you recently won this award." Or, "Hey, Mr. Jones, I saw your amazing article in *Advertiser Infomercial Monthly*, last month." By starting the conversation this way, you separate yourself from the crowd. They think, "At least this person researched me a little bit and knows who I am, rather than just sending me a cold, copy-and-paste email."

After your introductory message, you can move on to, "I'm a product developer, and I wanted to share a new product that I think would fit your product line in this category. If you're interested, let me know; I've got a video. The patent is pending, and I'd love to share everything with you."

The structure is very simple. We start by building a little rapport and demonstrating that we're professionals. We learned enough about them to start the email and get their interest so that we're not just like the other hundreds of generic emails they get every day. And then we cut right to the chase: "Here's why I think my product would benefit you. Here's where it would fit in your business." Now we've demonstrated that you're a professional twice, by showing how your product would fit in with their business.

Again, we're not doing a hard push. Either they're interested or not, so we send one message out, and then we go on to the next person. Since we're going to message a lot of people directly through LinkedIn, I would recommend building out your profile and updating it.

Do not call yourself "inventor" when you introduce yourself, because whenever anyone thinks of "inventor," they think of movies like *Back to the Future* or *Flubber*. Most people's stories about working with an inventor end in a bad story because inventors make products and then misadventures or business mistakes take place. Instead, you want to call yourself a "product developer."

Your updated LinkedIn profile needs to make it very clear that this is what you do. Instead of it saying that you're a high school teacher and this is your part-time job, it needs to look more professional, and there needs to be more congruency between your message and what you provided. They don't want to see this as a one-off invention. They want to see you as someone who's serious about what they're doing; you're more likely to have them want to see your video.

If you're not sure the person you found is the one in charge of new products, you could send a message that says something like, "I have a new product in this category, and I would like to submit it for review by your idea submission person. Who should I send my nondisclosure agreement to, or does your company have your own?" Most companies have their own NDA, so they'll want to use that; you just need to check it and make sure it meets your needs.

You also want to let them know that you've applied for a patent or trademark, so they know where you are in the process. By letting them know you have a working model with a video, you make it more enticing. A lot of these people get inundated with emails and messages about just an idea, but the person hasn't taken it through the process. They're only at step one of the Invent WOW procedure, whereas we've done much more; we have a working prototype and a video that we can show them, and we want to let them know we're not like other inventors. We're the real deal. We're product creators.

Once you go through this process, and they see your WOW IDEA, you'll move into the next phase, which is negotiations. The first phase is getting them interested.

The Negotiation

It's important to understand the financials of this business before you go in. If you have no idea what licensing deals are like, you can accept a percentage that's terrible without knowing it. You might also get offered something that's amazing and not know it, and therefore turn it down because you think it's too low. I want to give you some real information to help you with that.

I've seen percentages as low as 1 percent of gross. Depending on the way the deal is structured, you can make a whole bunch of money, but there are different pieces to each deal.

For example, when you license a product to a TV infomercial company, they're going to spend a couple of million dollars on TV advertisement to run their infomercial where everyone can see it. Their goal is to simply break even on the commercials, because for every person who sees that infomercial and buys, there are nine or ten more people who see that infomercial and don't buy on the phone, but if they see it in a store, they'll buy it. There's a very strong correlation between infomercial and retail sales, and that's very valuable for us. You can accept a very low percentage from TV sales but negotiate for a higher percentage of retail sales, where there's more profit available.

Most companies that aren't TV-based license at around one to two percent. They're in a similar range. However, I have seen licenses as high as five percent. If you have skin in the game, the further you go down this process through the Invent WOW system, the higher your percentage will be.

WITH EVERY STEP of the Invent WOW system, you diminish the risk of your potential partner. When you just have an idea on a napkin, there's a possibility that it won't even work when you build it. It's very common that an idea looks great on paper but doesn't work in the real world.

When you build your first prototype by hand, you've already lowered the risk a little bit, because now you've seen that it could work in the real world. As you go through your testing phase, showing it to people and building multiple versions, and move towards a final production-ready or good-looking product, you've lowered the risk a bit more. Now they know what the final product looks like and you have some feedback. As you perfect the design, test it out and start showing it to larger audiences, you lower the risk even more.

And if you go through what we're going to cover in the next chapter and do a crowdfunding campaign, you will demonstrate that people will actually pay for it, and you will have removed the highest level of risk. That's the biggest risk. You can have a great invention that people don't get or that just doesn't connect with them for some reason we didn't predict, and then the product fails. It can happen.

You can remove that risk with a crowdfunding campaign, because now you can say, "We've already sold this many units at this price point." That lowers the risk and increases the percentage you can ask for because you've changed the risk-reward balance for them.

Straight to the License

There are companies out there that might say to you, "Just create your drawings and go straight to the licensing stage." That business model is fine, but it limits how much money you'll make. Even a small crowdfunding campaign demonstrates that you're much more than just a drawing on a napkin. That means that they'll offer you a much higher percentage. They'll give you a much better deal because the product is already sold; people already want it, and they'll be eager to jump in.

This process all comes down to the product developer. How much money do you have available to take yourself through the Invent WOW process? Can you put together the resources to launch your crowdfunding campaign? If you can't, you may have to stop earlier in this process with your first invention and use the money from your first license to fund your next invention. You can work your way up to a higher percentage through multiple inventions.

Reflection Questions

1. How do you feel emotionally about the idea of giving someone else total control of your product? Would it affect you or make you feel like you were powerless if they changed the name, the color, or other parts of the design?

2. How does your emotional attachment to your invention or product relate to your financial desires? Are you willing to give up more control and let them change the product and rename it, as long as you start making more money? We have to balance these two things because I don't want you to be a sad millionaire.

3. Have you thought about the types of companies you'd like to license to and what you're looking for?

4. Write down some ideal numbers for you. What's your dream percentage? What's your dream licensing arrangement? What's your dream company? Let's predict a little bit here. We want to get as close to that as possible.

❖

Activity

Whether you're going to launch and build your own business or license, you want to understand the market that exists for your invention. When you look at a list of companies that create similar products, if you're licensing, they're your potential partners, but if you're going to make it yourself, they're your competition, and you want to advertise to their audience.

Either way, your mission for this chapter is to find all the companies that have a product line that your product would fit into, or companies that have the audience that you could sell your product to. A little bit of research goes a long way, and this information will help you no matter what you decide as you go forward.

Part two of this activity is if you want to license. When your product is ready, you're going to research and find the people you want to contact. Start by creating your new LinkedIn profile as a product developer. Then find the people at each specific company you're going to contact and message them, either asking for the right people to reach out to or reaching out to them directly using the templates I shared with you earlier in this chapter.

You may want to wait until you've read the next section before you make a final decision about licensing, but either way, do your research first and then join me in the next chapter.

12

THE LAUNCH

Twenty years ago, I met a high-energy guy full of ideas and with a passion for fitness; his name is Howard Panes. For a time, we were both working as personal trainers in New Jersey. He wanted to become an inventor like me and would constantly jump on the latest trends. He was always trying new ideas, like energy drinks when they were becoming super-hot. When the e-cigarette market exploded, he called me to ask if I had ever seen them. I told him I had and was not at all interested.

At my core, I'm a fitness guy, and I'm not into smoking – even if it's through a machine and supposedly "healthy." My mother passed away from lung cancer.

Fast-forward to a few years ago, and he created and built one of the top e-cig brands in the world, and then sold his business to a major tobacco company. He was looking for something new and called me with an idea for a new ab device, which became the Stealth Core Trainer. As I mentioned a few chapters ago, we started that project with a Kickstarter campaign. Not because we needed the money, but because it is the best way to get confirmation from the market that people want a product and are willing to pay for it.

Howard looked at social media and saw that "planking" was

getting popular again. People were taking pictures of themselves planking all over the world and in the most unexpected locations. The plank is an amazing isometric exercise, but staring at the ground, the most interesting thing you can see is a drop of sweat sliding down your nose onto the floor. Your mind gives up before your body.

We started to wonder if there was a way to make the plank interesting. The device we created is very simple: you place your phone on the Stealth Core Trainer and use it to control the games you play. When you perform a plank using this device, you last longer because your mind isn't thinking about the pain anymore. You can activate the part of your mind that enjoys games and feels pleasure.

Howard came to me with his vision and, based on his idea, I built the first prototype. I went through the entire Invent WOW process and continued to tweak the prototype until it was perfect. The initial prototype started out with a piece of plywood and a plastic dog toy. We modified the design, threw a phone on top, and started playing some downloaded games to see if you could control a game using your abs. That's the core of the WOW IDEA. It's not just about making the plank not boring; it's about making it fun! Using the prototype, I was training my abs and *enjoying* it.

Kickstarter is a powerful litmus test for an invention. It's a great platform to both validate your idea and raise the funds you need to launch it without having to sign a five-year lease on a brick-and-mortar building, putting your life savings on the line or giving up part of your company to an investor.

We received over two thousand pre-orders and were able to survey that audience. We interacted with each customer to find out as much as we could about them. The more we understand our customers, the stronger our business will become. We took that data and created "lookalike" audiences on Facebook to market our e-commerce store to people who were similar to our existing customer base.

The Stealth Core Trainer hit its tipping point while I was writing this book, so I wanted to include it as the final story in the book to show that I'm still following the Invent WOW method, and I believe that I will sell over a million units of this simple device.

We don't always want to give up control of our products. Sometimes you're excited about both sides of the business, especially if you're more of a businessperson and this is a one-off invention. If you want to pivot into making this your business, you may decide to go with the launch path.

I know some inventors are serial entrepreneurs, and they'd much rather do a licensing deal. Wherever you fall on the spectrum, understanding the process of the launch and how we put it together will help you make that critical decision. And the further you take your product down the launch path, the higher that license fee will be if you do decide to transition to the license, sell your company, or take a royalty.

Even if you are going to license your product eventually, there's a lot to be said for running a successful crowdfunding campaign before you enter negotiations. There are some initial costs with a crowdfunding campaign, so your financial situation may dictate the type of campaign you can run.

A crowdfunding campaign builds on the initial test – it's simply a way of raising money through pre-orders, rather than raising money from investors. It is a proof of concept, but it also gives you the money to build your business and product and set up production. When people hit that "pre-order" button, that validates your idea, and when you have enough of those pre-orders, it's time to transition from the initial test to crowdfunding.

Some people are tempted to skip the crowdfunding phase because they want to go straight to charging full price, or they have enough money to put into the production, so they don't need to raise pre-orders, or perhaps they feel a little bit overwhelmed by the process involved in crowdfunding. But crowdfunding, just like your $100 Facebook ads test, helps you to refine your price and create the perfect message. You will also be able to send a survey to your backers and get honest feedback.

You can think of crowdfunding as a deeper test of your product.

In the first test, people said they wanted to buy it and were prepared to place orders; now it's time for them to actually spend that money.

When designing a crowdfunding campaign, the most important component is the video. The more production value put into the video, the more successful the campaign will be. There are loads of companies that specialize in designing amazing crowdfunding pages and videos. For a small campaign, be ready to spend several thousand dollars. This investment will pay back tenfold when the orders start rolling in.

You can use the mailing list from your testing phase to get more information or to push for your first round of orders. If you are flying solo, you can create a survey with your initial ideas for pledge levels. Mail that survey to your pre-order list and give them the chance to give you feedback. They can help you dial into the levels that will be most successful.

While you can't change the overall message or any pledge levels once someone has pledged, you *can* add in new levels in the middle of a crowdfunding campaign. You can email the people who pledged at level one and offer them a specific bonus for upgrading to level two in the next twenty-four hours. Crowdfunding campaigns are very dynamic, and you can continue to tweak and improve throughout your campaign window.

Many first-time inventors think that Kickstarter is "set it and forget it" – that you can simply flip the switch and then turn off your computer for thirty days. Being proactive will help you to double or triple your raise and ensure that you are successful in hitting your campaign goal. You can continue to tweak that Facebook ads campaign and set up your crowdfunding page as the new target. Send your clicks to Kickstarter, or whichever platform you are using, and watch the pledges start to roll in.

Following a successful crowdfunding campaign, you can now transition into an online e-commerce store, which is very easy to set up these days. You can set up an account with Shopify for about $20 a month. They give you a whole pre-built website with all the templates in place and walk you through the process of taking orders and credit card details. You could be up and running in less than a day. And suddenly, you have a full-scale business.

There's this misconception out there that you need to have multiple products to have a business. That's absolutely not true. I have built many single-product businesses that have made six, seven, and even eight-figures. You can make massive amounts of money with a single product and a very simple e-commerce store. This is exactly how I built Stealth and some of my most recent businesses. This process is not just what I teach; it's what I do.

There are ups and downs when using Amazon as a sales platform. It's brilliant because you get access to a huge customer base, but the downside is that your profit is a little bit lower. They charge you a little monthly fee, and every time you make a sale, they take their cut. But the upside is access to a massive customer base and a chance to get a lot of reviews.

Every one of those reviews you get on Amazon becomes a testimonial that you can put on your own website. All that feedback is gold. As you begin to build your reputation via Amazon, when you have a good product name that's sticking in people's heads, when they go to your website, they will be willing to pay the exact same price, except you keep all the profit. That's the reason to have both your own e-commerce store and to sell on Amazon. You get access to the customers, but you also have the ability to make a little bit more money when people buy directly from you.

If you develop a great product and have some good intellectual property that can't be easily copied or replicated very quickly, you're going to have a constant and steady cash flow for years and years to come. And that's the whole Invent WOW concept of creating wealth: you get your taste of the American dream.

❖

Reflection Questions

1. Which part of the test and launch process makes you uncomfortable? You may be uncomfortable with the idea of building a

website or taking pre-orders for a product that's not built, or maybe it's the Facebook ads part that has you scared. Whatever part makes you uncomfortable, write that down here so we can face it together.

2. Where do you envision seeing your product? Do you envision seeing it as a crowdfunding campaign? Do you see it as something you sell through a Shopify store, an e-commerce store, or your own website? Or is it something you just want to sell on Amazon? Write down your vision for the product.

3. How does the thought of running your own business with a little money coming in every single day make you feel? Are you excited about the financial prospect or nervous about the technical process? Be aware of your emotions and communicate with yourself so that you can stay on track.

4. Does the thought of becoming financially successful and having control of your business make you feel good? I know it makes me feel pretty good.

Activity

There are several skills that we need to either acquire or master to create our tests and campaigns. We can either hire someone else to do them and utilize their skill, or we can learn ourselves. This comes down to your current financial situation. Running a Facebook ads campaign can be very cheap, but it might feel daunting if you are not familiar with it at all.

Your first step is to research the technology. Look at the different skills that you'll need to run your pre-test, your crowdfunding campaign, and your e-commerce store. Before you decide whether you can or can't do it, just make a list of the skills you need. What you certainly need is amazing pictures of the product, a good website design, and great sales copy. Work your way through the process we discussed in this chapter, and as you work your way through the list, for each skill, look at how long it would take you to learn it, and how much it would cost to bring someone else to do it.

A lot of people think website development will cost a lot of money, when really, for a nice-looking one or two-page website you're looking at under $500 to get it going. But you could also learn the process in less than a day, depending on how technical you are. You're a product developer, so maybe your time is best spent working on a different part of the business. Look at each of these skills and create your balance sheet.

Once you've completed your list, for each of these items, make a decision: "I'm going to learn how to do this, and I'm going to hire someone else to do that." Take your rough concept sheet and turn it into a series of action steps, so that you know your plan when you're going to go into a launch phase. Having an action plan and understanding which parts you need to hire out, knowing what that's going to cost, can also help you when you're planning out your finances. We want to be very fiscally responsible. Many inventors and product developers get too excited about the potential billions and don't pay attention to the early steps. We make a financial mistake, and suddenly we've run out of runway.

When you're factoring in the cost of your crowdfunding campaign, include these numbers so that all your costs are included in the total amount of money you're trying to raise through the crowdfunding campaign. We want the profit from the crowdfunding campaign to cover all the costs so that our business stays in the black. This is how you can build a business without taking any loss; you can outsource the risk to your customers.

THE MISSION

We've covered a lot of ground throughout the course of this book, but this is just the beginning. Creating, designing, formulating, launching inventions, and achieving financial success is a complicated process. You now have enough of a baseline to understand if this process is for you, and if you've made it this far, I have a feeling that it is.

I'm excited that you are not only an action-taker but also a finisher. There are loads of people who pick up this book and read the first chapter and never get any further, but the fact that you've made it this far inspires me and gets me excited. That's exactly why I took the time to write this book and share everything I know about creating WOW IDEAS.

I'm excited that we're on this journey together. This is a cooperative venture. If you reach out to me, I'll reach out to you. If you spend time with me, I'll spend time with you. I would love to hear about your ideas and inventions and see how I can help you grow your business.

You can use this book as a guide to take you through the process of succeeding as an inventor, and I'd love to hear about that. If I can provide guidance and mentorship, I want to do that. Please don't think that this is a one-way street.

If you came through this book and read it without participating in the activities, without going through the reflection questions, that's OK. Some people get so excited they just want to plow through the content. What I ask you to do now is to go back through, re-read each chapter, and dig into the activities. This will help you in the process of becoming a successful product creator.

My goal is not to sell books. I care more about getting my message out there than anything else. As you've seen, when I talk about real numbers, I've made a great living as an inventor, and I still have amazing inventions coming out. My business is not slowing down. What I care about is getting my message out there and helping new up and coming inventors to succeed and avoid the pitfalls that I fell into.

Now that we're in the final moments of this book, I have to send you out into the world with a mission, and what I ask you to do is to be active instead of passive – be an action-taker, and that means communicating with me. That means working on your inventions. That means following the steps in this book, and it also means in a few pages, when Amazon asks you if you want to leave a review for this book, you leave a real, honest review about your experience.

The great thing about writing books in the modern digital age is that I can continue to grow and improve. If there's something missing or something that you found a little bit confusing, you can email me, and I'll write you back right away; that will also help me to improve the quality of this book for people who read it after you, because every time you email me and tell me something in the book is missing, I'll add it in and publish a new version.

You can help the next version of this book and the inventors behind you. I'm really excited to see what you do. Your mission now is to get serious about your product creation and to share with me your ideas and help me help you. I want to work together with you.

I want to guide you and mentor you, and I want to see your success, so please *take action*. Let this book be more than just a few pages of inspiration. Instead, let it be a guide for changing your life. I believe that the fastest way to become a millionaire is to invent something great and launch it into the world. Infomercials and Kickstarter are the ways you can become a millionaire in less than a month in the modern world. I want your life to change, and I'm excited to see you cross the finish line.

You've taken the first step, and I'm very proud of you. The first step is often the hardest, so now continue your journey with steps two and three until you cross that finish line, when you can stand on the winner's circle, and I can proudly say that I've made yet another millionaire with the power of my book.

I can't wait to see your WOW IDEA on television, on the Internet, and wherever else you take it. I'm watching for you, and I can't wait to see your success. Thank you so much for being a part of this journey, and I'm proud of you for making it this far. I got my eyes on you, so let me watch you hit that prize.

ONE LAST CHANCE

Thank you for reading all of Invent WOW. As an extra bonus, I want to give you a free gift called the Crowdfunding Checklist.

This is the exact process I used to generate over $400,000 in sales on my last KickStarter. And it's yours free.

Just my way of saying thank you for grabbing my book ;)

InventWow.com/gift

FOUND A TYPO?

While every effort goes into ensuring that this book is flawless, it is inevitable that a mistake or two will slip through the cracks.

If you find an error of any kind in this book, please let me know by emailing:

support@inventwow.com

I appreciate you taking the time to notify me. This ensures that future readers never have to experience that awful typo. You are making the world a better place.

ABOUT DON BROWN

Inventor of the Ab Roller®

Don Brown is passionate about helping people achieve a healthier lifestyle and is the inventor of some of the most successful and iconic fitness products in history, including the Ab Roller® and Ab Coaster®, which revolutionized the way people perform crunches and abdominal exercises.

His love for fitness led him down the entrepreneurial path, becoming the founder of Xercise Inc. and co-founder of The Abs Company. Don aims to help others achieve success by sharing his journey and guiding people to help turn their WOW ideas into profits.

ONE LAST THING

Thank you so much for taking the time to read this. Although it seems like a very small thing, you have the chance to make a major difference in my life. Right now, the words from this book are fresh in your mind. And if you are reading this on an ereader, you will have an opportunity to leave me a rating or review on the next page.

It only takes a few seconds of your time, but it makes a major difference in my life. Without new reviews, books disappear from digital bookstores. It doesn't matter how many reviews you see from last month or last year, they don't mean nearly as much as your ten-second review from today. When you click that 5th star, it ensures that more people will see this book and have a chance to improve their lives.

It's a small step, but it has a major impact.

Sincerely,
    Don Brown
    InventWOW.com
    support@inventwow.com

www.ingramcontent.com/pod-product-compliance
Lightning Source LLC
Chambersburg PA
CBHW060844220526
45466CB00003B/1232